KT-579-093

# Portfolios Across the Curriculum and Beyond

WITHDRAWN

# Portfolios Across the Curriculum and Beyond

Donna J. Cole
Charles W. Ryan, Fran Kick

A00356

**CORWIN PRESS, INC.**
A Sage Publications Company
Thousand Oaks, California

Copyright ©1995 by Corwin Press, Inc.

All rights reserved. No part of this book may be reproduced or utilized in any form or by any means, electronic or mechanical, including photocopying, recording, or by any information storage and retrieval system, without permission in writing from the publisher.

*For information address:*

Corwin Press, Inc.
A Sage Publications Company
2455 Teller Road
Thousand Oaks, California 91320

SAGE Publications Ltd.
6 Bonhill Street
London EC2A 4PU
United Kingdom

SAGE Publications India Pvt. Ltd.
M-32 Market
Greater Kailash I
New Delhi 110 048 India

371.26 CoL
A 00356
EALING TERTIARY COLLEGE
ACTON CENTRE LIBRARY

Printed in the United States of America

**Library of Congress Cataloging-in-Publication Data**

Cole, Donna J.
    Portfolios across the curriculum and beyond / Donna J. Cole,
Charles W. Ryan, Frank Kick.
       p.  cm. —
    Includes bibliographical references.
    ISBN 0-8039-6403-X (cloth). —0-8039-6303-3 (pbk.)
    1. Portfolios in education—United States. 2. Educational tests
and measurements—United States.  I. Ryan, Charles W. (Charles
William), 1932-.  II. Kick, Fran.  III. Title.  IV. Series.
LB1029.P67C65   1995
371.2'6—dc20                             95-22649

This book is printed on acid-free paper.

95  96  97  98  99  10  9  8  7  6  5  4  3  2  1

Corwin Press Production Editor: S. Marlene Head

# Contents

# Preface

The issue of portfolio implementation within current teaching practices must be considered as we seek to reform the American education system. In this guidebook, we explain the purpose and rationale for initiating a portfolio process in the schools. A number of succinct reasons directed our efforts in assembling each chapter. They are the need to

1. Present professional educators with a clear rationale for portfolios in the school
2. Present realistic examples for portfolio implementation
3. Suggest alternatives to traditional assessment (i.e., paper and pencil tests)
4. Present portfolio examples by grade and subject
5. Provide ideas for enriching classroom practice
6. Stimulate professional educators to higher levels of performance

We are indebted to our public school colleagues for sharing with us their ideas and expertise relating to portfolios. We recognize the need for continued dialogue on portfolio use and development in public education environments. We hope that the ideas presented will stimulate further portfolio experimentation in the schools. We need to continue developing the portfolio process with preservice teacher candidates as we seek to develop strong partnerships with the schools.

We are indebted to Bonnie K. Mathies for her forward-thinking contribution of chapter 5, "Technology and Portfolios in the Future," and for providing a comprehensive list of computer software resources (Resource D).

We also would like to thank Jerry Herman for his initial encouragement and support for this project, and Gracia Alkema, president, Marlene Head, production editor, and Jamie Cox, marketing assistant, all of Corwin Press, for their expert care and handling of the manuscript.

Special thanks to Wright State University staff for editorial assistance: Vicki Miller for typing and stylistic editing and Missy Ratliff for typing and proofreading.

DONNA J. COLE
CHARLES W. RYAN
FRAN KICK

# About the Authors

**Donna J. Cole** has worked in K-12 systems in inner-city Cleveland and Chagrin Falls, Ohio, and in West Virginia and Utah. Her Ph.D. is in cultural foundations of education from the University of Utah, where she taught Introduction to Education and Social Studies Methods. She has been at Wright State University since 1987, where she coordinates the foundation phase of the teacher education program.

Dr. Cole's specializations are in cultural foundation (with a pluralistic thrust) and assessment (with a concentration on authentic assessment, especially portfolios). She cochaired the Ohio Consortium for Portfolio Development, which collaborated with Stanford University's Teacher Assessment Project, directed by Lee Shulman. During the 1993-1994 academic year, she was an associate with the National Network of Education, led by John Goodlad. As a result of this experience, Dr. Cole was instrumental in developing a partnership with the Fairborn Public Schools. As part of the partnership, the Professional School Teaching training program has placed interns in the classrooms and initiated a number of collaborative training activities with the school staff.

Dr. Cole has continued to contribute to the professional literature via articles, chapters in books, and teacher as well as student curricular guides. In her current assignment as Associate Professor and Assistant Chair of Teacher Education, she continues to teach and work for reform of teacher education.

**Charles W. Ryan** has served for the past 20-plus years in a variety of university posts and assignments that have required teaching and administrative responsibilities. From the role of Department Chairperson, he progressed to Assistant Dean and Dean of a major teacher education unit. His current assignment has required involvement at both the national and local levels in the politics of education and the development of strong undergraduate and graduate programs. In addition, Dr. Ryan has continued to conduct research as it relates to faculty productivity, organizational analysis, and career development theory.

Dr. Ryan's professional interests are wide ranging, and his most recent book, *Career Counseling: A Developmental Approach* with Robert Drummond, has been adopted by a number of counselor training programs. His career activities have interfaced with American public schools, colleges, universities, and state departments during a period that has witnessed significant changes in American education. He continues to teach and pursue scholarly endeavors while serving as Professor of Educational Leadership and Human Services at Wright State University.

**Fran Kick,** educational speaker and consultant, is the founder and coordinator of Instruction & Design Concepts, which services educational motivational leadership sessions and workshops. He is the creator and presenter of "KICK IT IN!" a dynamic and exciting self-motivational personal leadership program that demonstrates and gives examples of positive ways to deal with yourself and others. Since taking an educational leave of absence from teaching, he has developed his part-time speaking adventure into a full-time professional quest. Mr. Kick presents more than 100 instructional and motivational clinics and programs every year across the country to thousands of college/university, high school, and junior high/middle school students and the many professionals who work with them. He speaks at many state, regional, and national conferences, and his writing has appeared in numerous state and national educational publications. The U.S. Department of Education's Office of Educational Research and Improvement's ERIC/CAPS Clearinghouse has published Mr. Kick's work titled, "The Self Perceptions of Self-Concept and Self-Esteem" and selected it for inclusion in the Resources in Education Index. He has his B.A. in education and an M.A. in educational psychology.

**Bonnie K. Mathies** is Assistant Dean for Technology and Associate Professor of Education, Department of Educational Leadership, CEHS, Wright State University.

# The Road to Authentic Assessment and Portfolios

*Objectives*

After studying this chapter, you should be able to

1. Discuss evaluation's evolution into formal and authentic assessment
2. Discuss the basic rationale for authentic assessment procedures
3. Discuss the need for portfolio use in public schools
4. Describe the basic differences between process and product portfolios

## Introduction

Schools are state and local institutions mandated to educate future citizens. To educate can be translated into learning the basic knowledge, dispositions, and skills needed to exist successfully in the United States's structural democracy. Thus learning must be assessed, but documenting and assessing actual classroom learning has frustrated professional educators as well as the public during the last half of the 20th century. The national outcry for school accountability resulted in using standardized testing to document school learning, but tests fail to permit students to demonstrate what they have learned. Teachers refuse to accept a one-shot formalized instrument as the determinant of their teaching efforts and their students' learning. A formalized test appears rigid and static, a frozen task in time, as well as simplistic; it focuses on the final score, not on how the student arrived at the answer; and it promotes conformity, even though educators know students learn differently and at varying degrees. This dependence on exam results has led to tests driving classroom instruction, rather than the curriculum determining instruction within the school; the goal becomes excelling on the test. Individual student learning rests on how well he or she does on a test, rather than how much the student really knows and how the student might demonstrate the school content (inclusive of required knowledge, skills, and dispositions) in the most authentic manner.

## A Little Assessment History

The influence of testing on educational systems and policy appears more powerful now than at any time in history. However, nationwide school renewal efforts suffer from the counterdemand for test score improvement, and educational progress is undermined by the pervasive use of tests that contrast with current theory and practice. Evaluation, not a new concept in education, was evident when Socrates used mediated evaluations as part of his attempt to guide students' learning. But evaluation defined by testing can be traced to the Chinese (200 BC), who conducted civil service examinations.

Our nation's evaluation history is strongly rooted in the testing idea. Robert Thorndike (early 1900s), called the father of the educational testing movement, helped convince the country of the value of using testing to measure human aptitude. The standardized test paradigm gained momentum in the 1920s and 1930s.

The 8-year study by Tyler (1942) and the evolution of accreditation (the process of evaluating educational institutions) established formalized evaluation as the most substantial way to account for learning. Testing was identified as an important means of evaluation because a mathematical score (believed to be factual, thus true) could be exacted to represent learning. The establishment of the Educational Testing Service (ETS) in 1947 solidified the supremacy of tests as the ultimate assessment tool.

The 1980s theme of "accountability" fueled test use in documenting learning. School systems invested huge amounts of time, energy, and money in testing. Minimum competency tests, state-mandated tests, criterion-referenced tests, and norm-referenced tests were but a few that became an active part of the school schedule. These exercises involved limited tasks, for example, reading a phrase and answering a multiple choice item. A major testing criticism is that most exams require lower-level thinking skills, usually ignoring most higher-level—and perhaps controversial but certainly more useful—skills, such as synthesis. Almost every state expects educators to teach for overall content: knowledge, performances, and dispositions. Yet tests can give little or no information other than knowledge acquisition and basic skills. Although such traditional modes of assessment continue in the majority of classrooms, educators recognize the liabilities inherent with these tools.

The currently available state and national tests produce a shallow and unreliable picture of student achievement, do not correlate with school performance, and encourage unsound instructional practice. Teachers believe that the multiple choice format common to traditional assessment does not measure students' ability to organize relevant information or present a coherent argument. Teachers, when forced to teach to tests, understand that this leads to cheapened instruction, undermining the authenticity of test scores. Instruction falls to mere practice and drills, driving out quality teachers (Shepard, 1989). Traditional assessment practices lack sensitivity to the individual growth that educators desire in students; thus the instruction itself appears misguided (Valencia, Pearson, Peters, & Wixson, 1989). Educators know that reports based solely on traditional standardized test scores represent a limited, microscopic, and incomplete view of students' abilities (Hiebert &

Calfee, 1989) and fail to clarify the total progress of students (Flood & Lapp, 1989). As Wolf (1989a) explained, traditional assessment structure does not promote encouragement of lifelong skill acquisition, and much of the testing prevents students from thoughtfully responding to and judging their own work.

A solid assessment program consistently assists, as well as requires, students to take responsibility for record-keeping and metacognition and reflection while learning. Educational psychology theorists have generally viewed learning as interactive with a number of variables, and they oppose mere testing for accountability. Traditional, norm-referenced, competitive measures that rank students against one another (as letter grades or numerically scored tests) yield limited formative assessment information and seldom aid profitable instruction. For today's learners to be self-determining, they must self-monitor and self-evaluate. Constructive programs employ self-referenced growth measures designed to permit students to take ownership of their learning movement. Skilled evaluators base assessment on a developmental perspective. These evaluators marry growth development models with specific curriculum fields, such as reading stages, mathematical thinking, spelling, and so on. Rather than labeling students with arbitrary age or grade-level means, educators track each student's individual growth through developmental phases. Accurate assessment requires that teachers construct avenues of valuing, tracking, and recording individual factors, such as growth, improvement, effort, reflection, risk taking, change, and so on.

As we move toward the 21st century, educators are determined to validate usage of multidimensional assessment tools. Although informal strategies (e.g., interest inventories, checklists) were explored in the 1960s and early 1970s, educators and the public were not satisfied that these methods matched the dynamic processes involved in learning. The current cry for authentic assessment, in which documentation represents all aspects of learning, has surfaced.

Authentic assessment rests on systemic change. Thus educators are turning to the idea of authentic evaluation to demonstrate their students' learning progress. Please take a few seconds to reflect on the following ten educational thoughts.

*Ten Educational Thoughts*

1. Just because we taught . . . does not ensure that students learned.

2. Evaluation involves a set of tools used to analyze performance, including observation, demonstration, and work samples as well as tests.

3. Evaluation is subjective and judgmental.

4. Evaluation is a moral issue.

5. Evaluation should be both formative and summative.

6. Evaluation, to provide a clear picture, should include self-, norm-, and criterion-assessment criteria.

7. Evaluation, to provide a clear picture, should include aptitude and achievement test results.

8. Readiness and teacher instruction are significant factors to consider when evaluating.

9. The teaching goals should be considered when assessing learning.

10. Students need to be able to show what they have learned as well as what you want them to learn.

## What Is Authentic Assessment?

A fundamental authentic assessment principle holds that students should demonstrate, rather than be required to tell or be questioned about, what they know and can do. Hence authentic assessment usually is classified as performance based. When employing performance-based assessment, students demonstrate in a natural context what they have learned. This type of evaluation can be open ended, structured or unstructured, and announced or unannounced. Sound evaluation programs can provide, when needed, defensible student grades as well as test scores. Competitive, norm-referenced grading should occur with moderation and wisdom and is educationally most sound when used for helping the educator and learner develop a clearer idea of the areas in which the student needs to work.

Authentic assessment (AA), identified as a powerful evaluation idea, focuses on the desired curriculum outcomes. Therefore, actual, complex performances of reading, writing, researching, problem solving, creating, and speaking evidence must be included. Authentic assessment requires higher order educational outcomes in which students integrate their learning in realistic applications. Authentic assessment practices should encourage good instruction. Student evaluation needs to be a profitable use of time and should not distort or be harmful to classroom instruction. Authentic assessment aspires to equivocally support state-of-the-art instruction and curricula. When assessment interrelates with instruction, teaching becomes more effective. Therefore, AA must be integrated into instructional practices.

Several characteristics represent authentic assessment. Educators believe that assessment should measure student performance in relation to sound educational goals. The student should know these goals. Authentic assessment reflects observation of each student's current work. Because learning represents much more than merely retaining given knowledge and demonstrating a set of discrete skills, authentic assessment must include multidimensional indicators to include all the essential content identified by the system. Students apply skills, integrate knowledge, and demonstrate by acting on values and attitudes. Multidimensional instruments require the inclusion of various student performance indicators. A teacher must have available a rich repertoire of assessment strategies from which to select in orchestrating sensitive, student-appropriate evaluation activities for varying curricular disciplines. A few strategies include checklists, lab sheets, inventories, videos, tapes, interviews, and performance assessments. AA requires processing by student and teacher. Examples of this process include observation, conferencing, the use of the writing process, self-evaluation, and collaborative evaluation as well as traditional paper-and-pencil tests.

For maximum effectiveness, the total educational community must hold authentic assessment in esteem. Proper AA includes many different individuals working collaboratively to accurately evaluate student growth and learning. Incorporating multiple measures encourages examination of students' learning from varying perspectives; thus a more accountable picture of growth occurs. Each classroom might permit external assessment (district, state, or national tests), teacher-directed evaluations, student self-evaluations, and parental input, as well as input from other significant and informed parties. The exercises involved should be useful, worthy, and meaningful to students and the learning community. Students are held accountable for demonstrating learning. Likewise, educators provide students with informative feedback. Authentic assessment must be culturally, gender, and racially unbiased. Authentic assessment correlates with what students are learning and helps them gain confidence in their ability to master the subject.

---

### Authentic Assessment Components

Authentic assessment

- Must assist in learning
- Must encourage good instruction
- Must relate to curriculum outcomes
- Fosters higher order learning
- Follows developmental perspective
- Uses testing sparingly
- Supports time efficiency
- Reports meaningful information
- Promotes partnering of parents, educators, and students
- Fosters student metacognition and reflection
- Is individualized

---

Time, a precious and limited teacher resource, must be analyzed prior to undertaking AA. Educators should reallocate the considerable amount of time already sacrificed to assessment, evaluation, testing, grading, and record keeping. This reduced scoring time can then be redirected to saving and documenting student work.

Consider the following four ideas when planning to use AA.

---

### Four Important Authentic Assessment Ideas

1. The purpose of the activity should be clear. Instructors should know how they will use the results.
2. Instructors should design activities relative to instructional goals, asking students to apply what they have learned.
3. The activity should have more than one possible answer and perhaps more than one possible outcome.
4. Student-designed activities could serve as a possible assessment.

---

Authentic assessment of this nature develops within the school schedule. The assessment is administrated at various points during the students' progress, and a more comprehensive view of students' learning surfaces. Educators clarify what tasks students should undertake and how to perform them.

Scoring authentic materials causes concern in evaluation experts. Authentic assessment requires careful analysis, and instructors must keep written records. Educators decide if holistic or analytic scoring is appropriate for the evaluation purpose; establishing the scoring criteria before administration is essential. Both students and teachers must understand the task, purpose, and usability. All recording devices, such as checklists, rating scales, and scoring rubrics, must be available before the students undertake the activity. Although testing will be a part (usually limited), most of the assessment involves a process of unobtrusive information-gathering about students' learning. The assessment evidence being collected occurs during the course of the daily schedule and is ongoing (not just once or twice per grading period). The classroom environment should remain more student-learning centered. Students are questioned and observed, and their learning is explored. Because the educators will spend less time on standardized tests, efficiency is inherent in the design, and testing side effects should also decline. The following chart identifies a repertoire of authentic assessment strategies.

---

### Authentic Assessment Repertoire

- *Kidwatching/anecdotal records:* open-ended, narrative observational notes, logs, and records
- *Checklists:* structured, curriculum-anchored, observational guides, charts, and records
- *Interviews/conferences:* face-to-face conversations to access, track, and monitor student growth
- *Performance assessments:* criteria and instruments used for analytic scoring of complex performances
- *Classroom tests:* improving the construction and scoring of teacher-made achievement measures

all incorporated in a

- *Portfolio:* work samples, results, projects, video- and audiotapes, learning logs, student journals, and other pertinent student artifacts

---

The employment of portfolios has garnered significant attention as an alternative to traditional student assessment. There are several reasons why portfolios accurately attend to authentic assessment criteria.

## What Is a Portfolio?

Vavrus (1990) defines portfolios as "a systematic and organized collection of evidence used by the teacher and student to monitor growth of the student's knowledge, skills and attitudes" (p. 48). Portfolios can provide authentic and meaningful documentation of students' abilities. Curriculum, instruction, and assessment intersect via portfolios, tying the three together effectively for students. Portfolios must contain the artifacts of students' progress, as well as their reflections on both their learning and the chosen artifacts. Students must feel ownership of the portfolio, so they need to have decision-making power about the selected artifacts. Reflections assist them in taking responsibility for curriculum consumption.

Because students design the portfolio with the purpose of proving their learning, it concretely represents their efforts and accomplishments. This aids students in valuing themselves as learners as well as valuing their work. For students to assume responsibility, the portfolio must illustrate explicitly or implicitly the students' learning activities. The imperative portfolio ingredients are listed below.

---

### Imperative Portfolio Ingredients

- *Rationale:* purpose for forming the portfolio
- *Intent:* its goals
- *Content*: actual evidence of learning
- *Standards:* what is positive performance and what is unacceptable performance
- *Judgments:* what the content tells us about the student's learning

---

Portfolios contain actual classroom artifacts. Because the portfolio can contain many entries, both formal and nontraditional entries can be incorporated. Thus a full range of cognitive skills can be evaluated. The ultimate result will be reliable because of the availability of more than one illustration of academic performance. A clear advantage to portfolio assessment rests with the teacher's ability to evaluate the student's process of learning. Therefore, current learning theories can be identified and used. Built on this advantage is the involvement of the students in their own assessment. Students help in the selection of work samples and, even more important, reflect on what the selected entry represents. Students examine and analyze their work. This provides them the opportunity to reflect on the depth of their learning.

## Two Types of Portfolios

The portfolio might serve different purposes at different times of the school year. Two types of portfolios have surfaced. The primary and more active type of portfolio is the *process portfolio.* During the year, students should use the portfolio as a growth instrument. It needs to demonstrate students' performance at the beginning of a learning task. At this point, students should answer questions such as Why did you perform at that level? Where do you hope to move? How do you plan to get there? and When? As the students progress, teachers need to collect interim evidence to document the movement toward mastery. When the students successfully complete the task, the portfolio should include the final evidence. Once students master a task, they need to summarize what went into the learning task.

Even unfinished work might be placed in the portfolio to identify a problem area. The students then reflect on why it is a problem and what might be done about it. Wolf (1989a) explains that chronologically sequencing students' work and recording the macrogenesis (long-term evolution) provides a formidable view of the students' learning process. Most portfolios incorporate several projects, independent work, journals, and even formal testing results as pieces of the students' whole progression.

Because of the bulk and the time it takes to manage a process portfolio, eventually a metamorphosis should occur. From the rich and dynamic process portfolio, a leaner and more abbreviated portfolio can be produced that is called the *product portfolio.* The most realistic time for the reduction would be at the end of the academic year or at the completion of a program. The product portfolio should illustrate students' proficiency of the learning tasks. All selections should be materials that the student is willing to share and that reflect the student's success at mastering the curriculum. The school system should retain a copy of the product portfolio for future reference. To assist with higher levels of learning, the teacher should include summary reflective statements on how the student learns.

## Portfolio Contents

A portfolio will have multiple, but not conflicting, purposes. It should also include the student's personal goals, interests, and learning styles. Selections may also reflect the interests of teachers, parents, and/or the district. One almost universal portfolio purpose centers on showing the student's progress in the institution's instructional program (e.g., writing proficiency, mathematical competencies, etc.).

Because the portfolio should contain growth information, varying types of entries should be involved. For knowledge and skill mastery, the most obvious evidence is a series of student work samples (paper, tape recorder, or video) that shows improvement. For attitudes, changes observed on interest inventories, records, or outside activities could illustrate growth.

Portfolios have not yet become commonplace, so instructors need to provide samples of portfolios, reflective statements, and reflective questions to answer about entries. Teachers should identify the skills and techniques involved in producing effective portfolios. This requires a familiarity and comfort zone on the part of the instructor employing portfolio usage. As in all academic pursuits, an instructor makes or breaks the project. Enforcing the use of portfolios by disgruntled faculty will guarantee problems. Providing inservice for faculty members who desire authentic assessment strategies fosters success.

---

### What Portfolios Must Include

- Student-selected work pieces
- Student reflections on entries
- A clearly identified purpose
- Formative and summative samples
- Growth samples

---

## Planning for Portfolios

Before determining the utility of any instrument, teachers need to pay careful attention to its potential benefit. A few reasons for incorporating portfolios are listed below:

1. *Reflection of curriculum learned.* Portfolios are direct reflections of the actual classroom teaching. Portfolios relate directly to local standards, textbooks, and emphases.
2. *Discussion instrument.* Portfolios serve as a concrete vehicle for student-teacher, parent-teacher, and parent-student discussions.
3. *Comparison work.* Portfolios act as a cross-section lens, providing for future analysis.
4. *Variation of work.* A diversity of work sample results from portfolio construction. By providing various steps taken to complete the final work, the educator has evidence to identify the student's stumbling blocks.
5. *Assets and liabilities.* By viewing the total working patterns of the student, teachers can identify areas of strengths and weaknesses. Once identified, teachers can formulate strategies to use the student's strengths to assist in the problem areas.

If these suggestions are incorporated, the process of portfolio installation will be easier.

## How to Use Portfolios

For portfolio use in the classroom to produce positive results, careful preplanning must occur, including following several steps. First, the instructor must identify the ultimate goal of the project. The teacher must clearly articulate and discuss the goals with all school faculty. If goals are vague, portfolios become unfocused. It is important to identify the school's, district's, and state's goals that support classroom efforts.

Second, the educator must clarify the instructional strategies necessary to meet the articulated goals. Remember that portfolio usage reflects the curriculum and instruction that students receive. Teachers might complain that standardized tests do not test what is important or the curriculum used with students. Portfolios do. Opportunities need to be built into the curriculum via strategies to create artifacts for the portfolio. The artifact should emphasize the process employed to actualize the result, rather than right answers. By analyzing process, students acquire supportive evidence on their personal intellectual skills.

> *Reflection:* The quality of instruction directly determines the quality of the portfolio.

Third, once the instruction has occurred, instructors must determine growth. Assessment assumes a clear understanding of expectations and criteria. The evaluation should help the instructor systematically analyze what students have successfully accomplished and how they succeeded.

## Selecting Portfolio Content

To be effective, portfolios should contain a variety of materials so that the student, teacher, parents, and administrators can obtain an accurate picture of the student's development (Valencia, 1990). Students and teachers should be selective about what appears in the portfolio to ensure that the contents focus on the goals of the curriculum. A portfolio should include a table of contents, identification of who selected the piece, the date of the work, the description of the task, and student reflection on the entry. Students should have access to their own portfolios.

Once the content for mastery is identified, the student should make the initial selection. Teachers should provide guidance to the student about selecting the best work and clarifying why he or she has identified it as such. Teachers, as well as peer consultation, will assist students in making choices. Remember that permitting the students to build their own portfolios will foster their ownership.

The portfolio should include a variety of subjects and tasks. Realizing that portfolios serve as a biography of work and that they capture different snapshots of students' learning will help in the selection process. On a diverse project (such as a term paper), a collection of work throughout the project will aid in identifying the various intellectual tasks. Entries associated with attitudes and values are a must. This requires that the teacher include assignments assessing attitudinal data about learning, self-esteem, and career plans.

When assisting students in making their selections, teachers should give attention to choosing entries that demonstrate pre- and postgrowth. One suggestion is to have all students include some assignments for cross-group assessment. Because one of the longitudinal benefits of portfolios is for students to examine their approach to learning as well as their strengths and liabilities, teachers should guide students in including entries that will permit the benefits to happen.

Selection should start early in the year (entries from the previous year may be available). Continue to request selections of entries through units and at the end of a project. End-of-grading-period samples and end-of-the-year entries are imperative. Predetermined selection dates make the process progress smoothly.

---

### Possible Portfolio Artifacts

1. Work samples
2. Letters
3. Sketches
4. Drawings and paintings
5. Snapshots
6. Projects
7. Videos
8. Tapes
9. Checklists
10. Logs,
11. Tests
12. Computer work
13. Unit work
14. Collaborative projects and assessment from peers

## Reflection

Because the most desired outcome of portfolio construction is to have students assume learning responsibility and develop a desire to do their best work, it is essential to have reflective statements within the portfolio. Students need to develop metacognition, the ability to think about their thinking. Students should examine the process involved in learning as well as the product. The goal of metacognition is to help students achieve self-actualization. Although immediate reflections might appear narrow or even shallow, continued reflection will lead to deeper insights. Portfolios will start to take on a new value. They will be the students' own history of who they are and where they have traveled in learning. Reflection, a tool for analysis of learning and self-growth, should begin early in a student's education.

The instructor must understand reflection and be a reflector in order to guide others. Students must understand that reflections are not summaries, but are serious writing activities addressing their learning. Summaries merely abbreviate what is evident in the entry. Reflections analyze and synthesize knowledge, skills, and attitudes as they develop. Reflections answer the following types of questions.

---

### Reflective Entry Questions

1. Why is this your best work?
2. How did you go about accomplishing this task?
3. What would you do differently if you did a task like this again?
4. Where do you go from here?

---

*Reflection:* Students seldom are requested to reflect on conventional assessment.

---

When preliminary work entries appear in portfolios, students reflect on each step of the learning process that leads to completion.

Students gain knowledge and understanding of "the scope of what they learned" (Wolf, 1989a, p. 39). Although original reflections might focus on less significant dimensions, such as neatness of showmanship, with practice, students develop the ability to modify and expand their criteria and factors. Students and teachers need guidance in writing reflective statements. According to Killion and Todnem (1991), we can categorize reflections in three directions.

---

### Three Reflective Directions

1. First, *reflection-on-action* requires looking back on what one has accomplished and reviewing the actions, thoughts, and product.

2. The second form of reflection is *reflection-in-action.* In this activity, the individual is responsible for reflecting in the act of carrying out the task. If, for example, the student is writing a story and has left out the setting, reflection-in-action could guide the correction of a major component of story writing.

3. The final reflective form centers on *reflection-for-action.* This reflection form expects the participant to review what has been accomplished and identify constructive guidelines to follow to succeed in the given task in the future.

---

## Reflective Teachers and Administrators

---

*Major assumption:* In authentic assessment, it is imperative that teachers reflect.

---

Teachers in an authentic assessment environment do reflect. According to Lasley (1992), "A teacher's level of experience will influence his or her ability to reflect critically. Neophyte teachers will not exhibit the same capacity for critical reflection as would be possible for a more veteran teacher." Dewey (1904) attends to reflective ability when he discusses "habit of reflection." Teachers should know how to teach and know how to reflect on the techniques used in classrooms. Reflective teachers, Dewey adds, are freed from engaging in impulsive or routine action.

A reflective teacher will be able to lead in our reformation of schools. Posner (1985) argues, "Reflective teaching will allow [the teacher] to act in deliberate and intentional ways, to devise new ways of teaching rather than being a slave to tradition, and to interpret new experiences from a fresh perspective" (p. 20).

Van Manen (1977) described a conceptual focus on critical reflection. He identified three levels of critical reflection:

---

### Van Manen's Reflection Levels

1. The first level centers on *technical criteria*. At this level, reflection is concerned with thinking about what techniques were used to achieve the stated objectives.

2. The second level involves *conceptual reflection*. The conceptual level focuses on the relationships between the instructor's practices and the theoretical principles guiding the practices.

3. The final level, *ethical reflection*, enables. The goal of a teacher-preparatory program designed to make reflective teachers would be to move preservice educators from a how-to perspective to discussing reflective decision making. Hence, to be a reflective instructor, one should assess the consequences of actions and determine ethical, political, and moral implications for schooling and learning.

---

Other theorists, such as Kitchener and King (1981) and Ross (1989), have even constructed developmental typologies to describe reflection. Their developmental approach suggests that teachers progress through stages of development. To constructively assist students with reflection, an instructor must become proficient at asking leading reflective questions. Wellington (1991) highlights several reflective questions:

---

### Wellington's Questions

- What did I do?
- What does it mean?
- How did I come to be this way?
- How might I do things differently?
- What have I learned?

---

Reflective teachers look at techniques and face frustrations to improve instruction and help students learn. As the instructor reflects more, assignments given to students will lead to more reflection. Thus a reflective teacher nurtures reflective, exploring students.

Reflections allow students to track their progress by reviewing their work throughout the year. Students who review their work over time also can see how their thinking and working processes have improved.

A concern that is typically voiced questions whether student reflections can and should be assessed. The answer is yes. Teachers must write back to students guiding their reflectivity. For example, "Chad, you did a fine job of summarizing the selection. Explore what you are now confident in doing. What will you do to enrich the activity in the future?" It does take time, but certainly it is time well spent, both morally and educationally.

It is important that school administrators develop their reflective skills in relation to school goals, as well as learning outcomes, administrative practices, and public needs for accountability.

To initiate portfolios, a preliminary assessment can determine the adequacy of the physical construction. A checklist or criteria-building list would help the student understand what must go into the design. Once the portfolio construction is finalized, then the remaining evaluations should be directed toward reflecting and mastery of the knowledge, performances, and dispositions.

Some portfolio advocates believe that formal tests should be eliminated from the portfolio. Rather than viewing formal and authentic as polars, our view rests on the idea that authentic assessment actually bridges standardized testing with class assessments.

Within the portfolio, a student should have standardized test results with reflective statements.

## A Word on Assessing the Portfolio Itself

Two givens are identified when discussing the evaluation of the portfolio.

*Given 1:*  Authentic assessment means eliminating the old way of thinking.

*Given 2:*  The primary success of evaluation is allowing students to take ownership of their learning.

Regarding Given 1, when discussing authentic assessment, one must be willing to accept that this type of evaluation is truly authentic and breaks away from the restraints of traditional assessment. The old paradigm wherein you could put a letter grade, a point system, and so on as the final statement on students' efforts and learning is rejected. Traditional measures can be a part of the process but never the only, and surely not the final, word.

Given 2 rests on the premise that for too long, teachers have accepted the responsibility for student learning. Teachers were responsible for knowing how each student learned and were expected to make learning occur with each student. It did not work, did it? Why? Because students were relieved of the responsibility of accounting for their own learning. The public was paying for their free public education, and educators were being held responsible for their learning. Thus they were free to act as resisters, as if the whole program was their opponent. Their job was to challenge the actual act of learning. To deactivate this faulty paradigm, the multidimensions of evaluating portfolios follow.

First, in the planning stages, multiple scoring strategies must be decided on. Instructors must detail what types of assessments will occur and when. What will be the place of formal assessments? Will you require students to have formalized tests within the portfolio? Remember, it is all right to use traditional assessments, especially for having students see how they score compared to each other. It also helps them reflect on their test-taking skills and behaviors.

Second, to get the portfolio established, a checklist or point sheet can be devised to bring all students on-line. This might sound a little behaviorist, but our view is that an instructor must use all types of learning theories to accomplish the learning task.

More educational specialists are accepting authentic assessment as an appropriate source for documenting the learning process. Authentic assessment intends to involve students in challenging evaluations that approximate, or at least better represent, the assessments likely to face them as professional citizens and consumers (Wiggins, 1989). The actual evidence for assessment refers to the context and content in which a learned task results. This evidence can be designed to represent real situations, problems, and concerns and, more important, can involve students in the actual assessment process. Because educators are required to teach for the advancement of knowledge, performances, and dispositions, it follows that assessments should also provide evidence that students have made progress in obtaining content knowledge, skills to activate the information, and attitudes to ensure the use of the given knowledge and skills.

## Summary

The key to making portfolios work rests in learning how to adapt the portfolio to varying age, motivational, and ability levels of students. Portfolios offer teachers and students numerous benefits. They document students' growth, change, and risk taking, and they can be adapted to any grade or motivational level. They provide both a wide-angle and narrow-angle view of the student. As Margie Krest (1990), an English teacher who has used portfolios for 6 years, explains,

Thus over the past six years, the portfolio has become a vital part of my . . . classes. Because it is so adaptable, I enjoy using it and seeing the students motivated to strive for the grade they desire. . . . And most important, as I've used portfolios,

I've realized the extent to which the portfolio system is consistent with the theory behind the emerging paradigm [that] reflects a strong, student-centered [class]. (p. 34)

In chapter 1, a rationale and purpose of portfolios as a form of nontraditional assessment was provided. Also, a link to portfolios and the educational reform movement was highlighted. Chapter 2 will present portfolio assessment in a nontraditional format. In Chapter 3, a number of portfolio models illustrate varying subject matter possibilities for systematic infusion in schools. A portfolio process to assist teachers and administrators with personal professional growth is outlined in chapter 4. Chapter 5 looks toward the future as technological possibilities for portfolios are discussed.

# Implementation Strategies for Portfolios

| | |
|---|---|
| | **Objectives** |

*Objectives*

After studying this chapter, you should be able to

1. Develop a process for informing parents and community agencies about portfolio plans in your school

2. Develop a plan for starting portfolios at the building or unit level

3. Develop strategies for assessing the impact of portfolios on student learning and teacher use

## Introduction

A portfolio process in the school requires a concerted effort to inform a variety of interested groups, such as parents, community representatives, administrators, school board members, and all teachers. It is essential that each school generate guidelines for informing others of their portfolio plans and general results. Systemic infusion of a portfolio process across all subject areas will generate a pool of information of interest to parents and teachers on each student's learning style, self-esteem, and educational plans.

Infusion is defined as a process in which the traditional curriculum is integrated with other learning efforts (e.g., portfolios). Traditionally, students have completed work sheets, term papers, book reports, oral reports, and paper-and-pencil tests. Portfolio assessment as infused promotes the concept that learning is student centered and the responsibility of each learner. Portfolio use requires the student and teacher to meld traditional curriculum efforts with reflective analyses of the learning process. In short, systemic infusion describes the process whereby all teachers implement the portfolio process in those subjects currently taught in the schools.

In seeking to implement a portfolio process, each school community will need ample opportunity to plan how they wish to redesign their student assessment effort and how these plans will take shape over a period of time. Also, a shared decision-making approach must be developed that establishes connections between students, families, communities, and their schools. A reciprocal exchange of ideas on the purpose of education and how students are to be assessed will then develop. This dialogue must be genuine and occur on a frequent basis so that all those interested in accountability will understand the process and purpose of learning. As suggested earlier, we must move beyond measuring student growth through scores on standardized tests and develop insights into the total process of learning and how people use a number of approaches to master academic and social interaction skills (Flood & Lapp, 1989).

Measuring student growth through standardized tests is an established venue, but we must empower teachers, school counselors, and administrators to develop additional strategies and processes for assessing student growth. In this way, accountability to the community will be demonstrated and provide additional evidence that our schools are doing a fine job of educating future adult citizens. The implementation of a portfolio process provides a construct for shared accountability and a vision of the future that includes high-quality education for students in a particular community (Mills, 1989). It involves parents, community members, and civic organizations along with appropriate state and university agencies in assuming some responsibility for assessing the total growth of students.

What we are seeking through a portfolio process for authentic assessment is information sharing on a regularly scheduled basis as well as informal opportunities for reporting to all constituents information about student progress. As suggested, portfolio analysis and reporting will extend beyond test scores to include substantive descriptions of what students are doing and experiencing in terms of program, curriculum, and teaching efforts. The portfolio will also discuss student access to broad-based school opportunities in curriculum, sports, and subject-specific clubs. The portfolio will document academic progress in addition to identifying elements of effective citizenship, such as the development of coping skills that permit one to live and achieve success in a democratic society. As was suggested, methods of communicating to parents and the public will include exhibitions of student work, such as displays and demonstrations of what they have learned and accomplished. The portfolio can provide this unique link between the classroom teacher and the students who participate in those planned learning activities. The portfolio process of communication must be collaborative and provide opportunities for the education community to inform citizens in the community of school-based learning activities.

To implement a portfolio process will require reallocation of funds from the school budget as well as increased external support from the community. One approach is to provide community grants to schools that successfully start a portfolio process that documents what students are learning. This process can help teachers develop, document, and share their practices with the community and also reward excellence in teaching. Certainly, the local business community should be involved in the development of an award system that recognizes teachers' efforts to improve the quality of learning through a portfolio process. Implementation, then, will depend on the development of a school-based portfolio as a well-established process in grades K-12 and complete commitment by the teachers and administrators of a particular school or building.

A reform of this magnitude will be accomplished by local and state-based mandates to improve the pedagogy that occurs in American public schools. It will require teachers and administrators to reflect on and analyze their educational practices and to develop alternative assessment strategies. Naturally, the provision of useful knowledge and information to assist students in coping in a technological world is important, but the curriculum will change only when educators carefully consider what they are seeking to do and under what conditions. In implementing a portfolio process, teachers and interested school faculty will need time to engage in those essential activities that lead to substantive curriculum and assessment reform.

## Reporting Portfolio Progress to School Personnel

In more traditional learning environments, student progress is reported at 6- to 8-week intervals—this process will no longer suffice in a society of rapid change. In the future, students will enter and exit the school at different time periods after mastery of selected content. Traditional June graduations will be replaced by differential entry and exit points for students, and the portfolio will permit continuous documentation of learning over the calendar year.

Throughout the 12-month school year, parent-teacher-student conferences will provide opportunities to review student progress. They will also permit planning of educational needs for each student in academic, self-esteem, and career areas.

In planning for the reporting of student progress to parents and administrators, the following guidelines will be of help.

1. *Develop an overview of portfolio efforts with student work samples.* Parents and administrators will need an executive summary of the portfolio and an explanation of what it contains. A product portfolio evaluation form used by the teacher will be of help with this conferencing (see Resource B).

2. *Present the total portfolio process used in a given grade or subject area.* It is important for all interested audiences to recognize

the range of subject matter presented in a portfolio in contrast to a single test score.

3. *Present the portfolio content as evidence of the student's growth in all subject areas.* It may be necessary to simplify the reporting process and concentrate on a selected subject or two.

4. *Present the portfolio evidence as part of student growth and development as a person.* It is easy to fall into the trap of reporting success stories, but it may be more valuable to illustrate the difficult process of mastering the English language, mathematics, or science.

## Planning for Reporting

Throughout this guidebook, we have emphasized the process portfolio and suggested content for inclusion. It is now imperative that a plan for conferencing with students and reporting to other interested groups be detailed. The purpose of portfolio use must be repeated consistently over time if the implementation of this innovation is to succeed. In reporting to all individuals, the value of portfolios must be summarized and graphically illustrated. We suggest the following basic steps for developing a reporting system:

1. Identify the subject(s) to be reviewed prior to the conference with student or parents.
2. Use a portfolio conference review sheet (see Resource B).
3. Discuss student learning styles in relation to selected portfolio entries.
4. Establish dates, times, and location for student or parent conferences.
5. Summarize the conference results (see Resource C).
6. Review school policy statements for release of student data.
7. Consult with the school administrators about conferencing plans.

The above guidelines imply both a political and policy awareness that is essential for reporting student data to constituency groups.

## Reporting to Administrators

The administrator's role in developing a portfolio program involves both public and school-based support. Support can range from policy interpretation and administrative approval to budgetary allocations for materials or training. In the development of continued support, the faculty must provide data of portfolio use in assessing student growth. The portfolio provides evidence of curriculum implementation and student growth across various subject fields.

We suggest monthly conferences with the building administrator on portfolio use, evaluation, and problems. This can be accomplished by individual faculty conferencing with the administrator or teams by subject, grade level reporting on issues, and so on. If the administration conducts monthly faculty meetings, we recommend portfolio updates as an agenda item.

It is extremely important that learning goals and curriculum standards used in the school be produced to inform and drive curriculum development and assessment standards within each school. The administrator's role is critical in assisting and providing leadership for organizing curriculum content, establishing performance standards, and assisting staff in defining the major areas of study and competencies that students must demonstrate prior to graduation. Administrators must be the link that will assist teachers in informing parents of portfolio practices and revised assessment strategies. Along with this goal, performance indicators for success in each particular school should concretely describe what students should be able to do to meet either local or state standards for graduation. Administrators should consider the following guidelines in assisting the development of a portfolio process:

1. Provide guidance to staff for local curriculum development.
2. Generate an educational vision of important learning goals to be developed and what the purpose of learning is in the school.
3. Assist teachers in reporting students' learning and their abilities to a) demonstrate understanding of core curricu-

lum concepts and b) think and reason across a wide range of learning activities. In addition, assist teachers in generating real-life situations and assisting students to apply knowledge in dealing with them.

4. Foster teacher instruction that nurtures students' imagination and creativity in a number of learning domains.
5. Support teachers who use a range of teaching strategies and assessment processes to report diverse ways of learning and performance.
6. Encourage all school staff to use portfolios, and enlist the aid of support people (e.g., the librarian, media technologist, school counseling staff) in linking student portfolio work to their goals and objectives.
7. Develop a plan for comprehensive information gathering on local assessments that will be in concert with state mandates and community needs.

These efforts by the administrator will lead to an effective portfolio process.

## Reporting to Parents

As we seek to improve and increase parental involvement in the learning activities of the school, a key factor will be established—partnerships with parents. Teachers and administrators must take an active role in seeking parent or legal guardian involvement. A critical variable is the sensitivity of school staff to parents' feelings of isolation from school. We must help them overcome their feelings of inadequacy about the learning process and feelings that we do not value their input. Communication between both groups must involve regular meetings and a flow of information via letters or newsletters to the home. In fact, why not develop a parent team to help compose, edit, and distribute a school newspaper?

Teachers, working in groups, should develop plans to communicate with parents through traditional forms, such as newsletters and telephone calls, as well as through technology, such as electronic mail, FAX notes, and Internet linkages. The reporting of student progress can be more fully explained via narrative analyses—it permits fuller documentation of how students learn and a description of each teacher's expectations (Valencia, 1990).

Another approach is to provide parents with a weekly plan of curricular goals, homework requirements, grading practices, and ideas for parents to help their children with school learning activities. Supplementing this approach with adult teacher aides in the classroom increases the involvement of adults in the learning process. The time has come for parents to assist in the teaching of our nation's youth—it is a shared responsibility. However, school staff must be aware that parents work and often have other children at home, thus precluding active involvement in school activities. The use of electronic mail or voice mail permits brief messages about their child and school work requirements.

The increased use of parent-teacher-student conferences is a viable process for improving and increasing parent involvement in the school. A survey of parental working patterns, interests, and special or unique talents builds a file of potential classroom aides or volunteers. This file provides a resource for classroom tutors, mentors, and teacher aides. It also increases parent involvement in the school activities of their child.

Parental support of school programs is often increased when parents understand the learning goals established for their children. Plan to discuss student learning activities in several subject areas, but be cautious in reviewing the total academic program of the student. Parental confusion could result from an information overload. It is suggested that you focus on areas where learning needs attention, such as writing, mathematics, or science. Rotate discussions from one conference to the next.

Samples of student work over time, such as a grading period, should be presented. Discuss student growth, or lack thereof, with specific illustrations from the portfolio. Help parents grasp the significance of reflectivity and student ownership of learning. Point out how important it is for students to develop as learners with parental support. A portfolio conference report (see Resource B) will assist you with this conference. As suggested by Farr and Farr (1990), the parent conference provides a unique opportunity to showcase your plans for helping the students become more effective learners.

A number of parents will emerge as articulate supporters to assist in moving to authentic assessment. Portfolios will provide a bridge to aid parents in understanding the multidimensional aspects of learning evaluation. As advocates for a broader form of assessment, parents form a vital bridge with the school board and other elements of the community.

## Reporting to the Community

A number of interested constituency groups have a strong interest in school activities (e.g., sports, plays, debate, arts) and in learning-achievement test scores. The portfolio provides an excellent opportunity to report student learning activities in a nontraditional format—that is, authentic assessment of curriculum goals and practice within the school system. We suggest the following ideas for presenting portfolio results:

1. Portfolio-based science fairs open to the community
2. Electronic portfolio demonstrations to the school board
3. Portfolio displays at shopping malls, public buildings, and selected business sites

Faculty should consider this effort as part of school public relations to inform the community of school activities. A student's portfolio should present a balanced portrayal of his or her growth in academics, extracurricular activities, and civic and social skills.

## Summary

In this chapter, a number of suggestions have been presented to assist faculty and administrators in implementing portfolios. While developing portfolios, it is important to include other concerned partners in the learning process.

# Using Portfolios
# in the Classroom

*Objectives*

After reading this chapter, you should be able to

1. Develop a procedure for portfolio use in the classroom
2. Develop a model portfolio for the students
3. Develop alternative assessment procedures for the classroom
4. Develop a plan to share student learning growth with parents

## Using Portfolios in the Classroom

As the national school reform movement continues to gain momentum, the American schoolteacher searches for new approaches to enrich student learning and improve instructional content within the classroom. One avenue for this endeavor is the use of student-based portfolios for learning and documentation of developmental growth over a 13-year period of time for students in grade K-12. The student portfolio provides a continual record of student learning activities in each school year and evidence of developmental growth as it relates to a particular subject area. The portfolio provides tangible, concrete evidence—needed by teachers and others interested in a child's learning—that this has occurred (Wolf, 1989b).

Portfolios in the classroom promote student-teacher collaboration in planning learning activities. It is a time for reflection on the part of both parties on the purpose of school. The classroom serves as a natural environment for the infusion of innovative learning. The portfolio can be a vehicle for this change.

In developing a classroom process for the use of portfolios, one must articulate a variety of steps that will communicate to students your learning expectations and plans for the portfolio. Students must understand their responsibility for self-learning and commitment to maintaining the portfolio during the semester or academic year. A major tenet of portfolio use involves students' becoming more thoughtful regarding their selection of work for inclusion (Vavrus, 1990). When this occurs, students will begin to self-select learning activities that help them understand what they have learned in the classroom. In developing a model for the classroom, the following considerations can be helpful for planning.

---

### Classroom Considerations for Implementing Portfolios

1. Decide which curriculum objectives are to be related to the portfolio, and have students insert content materials in that area.

2. Use expandable folders or three-ring notebooks with plastic sleeves to store portfolio contents.

3. Establish rules for housing portfolios. (Some teachers do not want them to leave the classroom.)

4. Develop a cover sheet or table of contents that outlines information found in the portfolio. This will be particularly helpful in parent or student conferences.

5. Develop a regular time period for examining portfolios and rating the content within.

6. Include a variety of assessment procedures as you score the portfolios or grade them. Most teachers seem to prefer assigning a grade to the portfolio.

7. Require students to select at least one or two pieces of work per week or grading period for insertion in the portfolio.

In dealing with particular content areas, a variety of activities have proven helpful. It is important to collect work samples and evaluate student development over a period of time for any learning activity. For example, in science, students could write a preliminary paper on what they know about an upcoming topic, conduct an experiment, keep lab notes, and give a summary report of their findings as portfolio evidence. In language arts, document and provide some evidence of accomplishment in grammar, spelling, sentence construction, paragraph writing, and so on (Carr, 1987). Other content evidence for social studies, art, and English should be included.

## Portfolio Plans for the Classroom

Because portfolios are part of a developmental process, simply documenting the work that students do is not enough. All teachers must ask, "What do I want to accomplish by using portfolios in my classroom?" as they develop the process. In answering this question, it will be helpful to define the content of the portfolio as it relates to documenting student progress, instructional support, and communication avenues with administrators and parents. A key factor is the use of portfolios to document learning and social growth over time. Portfolios tell us what students have learned and how they learned it as they participate in learning activities. Students need to understand their own intellectual history as it relates to spending 13 years in the public school. It also assists teachers in analyzing their own particular teaching strategies and performance over time.

Portfolios help link instruction, learning, and assessment into an interactive model that reflects on each area of study in a positive way. Portfolios will emerge from a teacher-initiated curriculum rather than one based only on traditional testing. In essence, a more powerful curriculum than just isolated skills as measured by subject matter testing will emerge.

## Purpose of Portfolios

Portfolios can be used in conjunction with performance-based assessment of students. They will contain samples of students' work collected over a period of time. Generally, teachers and students work together in determining items that will be included in a portfolio. Items are placed in the portfolio at regular intervals, and evaluation is a continual process. Both student and teacher must reflect on items to be selected and included as part of the assessment of growth and learning.

Portfolio use is rapidly growing in popularity throughout the United States; a couple of state school systems (Vermont and Kentucky) have mandated portfolios for use in Grades K-12 to assess learning. As an alternative to traditional student assessment, portfolios provide the opportunity to assess the following:

- Student classroom work as documented over time
- Student cooperative and social skills that are not assessed through traditional testing
- Student growth in several academic content areas
- Student learning processes, not just test-based-outcomes assessment
- Student learning in a variety of areas (e.g., preparation for learning, sample drafts, and final product)

In addition, portfolios provide information important to teachers, counselors, school psychologists, and administrators regarding a child's performance over time, rather than just isolated fragments.

Also, documentation will be observed on learning habits in relation to study skills, task completion, and task assessment. In sum, portfolios provide a much broader and sweeping assessment of student learning and document the evidence so that it can be reviewed at annual interview evaluations with teachers and parents.

## Selecting Portfolio Content

The development of portfolios in a specific classroom or across grade levels will require teachers to decide which content areas will be included in the portfolio. Typically, teachers preferred to focus on language arts, art, music, and mathematics. However science and health and physical education are being included in portfolios. In general, portfolios should include content covering a variety of items, such as:

- List of books read
- Audio- or video-tapes of student learning in various situations
- Record of group reading, group learning activities, oral presentations, and student-conducted interviews
- Written reports
- Videotapes of work
- Graphs, charts, and diagrams
- Student development notes related to projects
- Writing and work samples

The content of portfolios usually involves a selective array of subjects that refer to student activities conducted within the classroom. Reports, letters, drawings, diagrams, photographs, videotapes, reading logs, classroom tests, unit projects, and computer work are typically found in portfolios. In the language arts area, students should select two or three of their best pieces of work during each grading period for inclusion in the portfolio. Work from other courses or subject areas could be included on a selective basis. Critical to inclusion of work in the portfolio is a self-evaluation or reflective comment on each chosen piece by the student. The final product at the end of the grade period or academic year should include representative samples from the year that show developmental growth.

Reflections by students on their work must be included in the portfolio. Each content area to be included should be reflected on, and students should be asked to justify their selection of material to be included. A student's portfolio may have distinct sections representing language arts, math, music, or social studies. Research efforts have indicated that most teachers prefer a single content area at the beginning of portfolio development (Cole & Ryan, 1995).

In determining the content area for portfolios, teachers will need to respond to several critical questions. For example, what will other audiences want to know about student learning? Will the included documentation show aspects of student growth that test scores don't capture? What types of evidence will best display student progress toward identifying school learning goals? Will the portfolio present progressive developmental evidence of student growth? When satisfactory answers have been determined by faculty and administration, you can then decide on a particular model or process to use for your portfolio. In Appendix A, a number of issues regarding portfolio development are cited for discussion.

## Suggested Portfolio Models

In developing the following material, we have relied heavily on field-based experiences with several school systems in southwestern Ohio to develop portfolio models for use in selective grades. The students involved were in Grades 3 to 7 and Grades 9 to 12 in an alternative high school. The students represented a typical school-based population and included minority representatives within the metropolitan area population. Portfolios were developed through careful teacher and student planning over a period of time. Faculty need to reflect and determine what specific content they wish to include in the portfolio for initial start-up activities. Also, evolutionary development will occur as students begin to put materials into the portfolio.

As teachers seek to develop a model for use in their classrooms or schools, the following types of questions should be addressed: What is your personal belief system regarding student learning? What do you believe the school experience should be? What is the goal of the teacher in facilitating student learning? What content area(s) must be recorded over time to show developmental learning? In addition, knowledge of the community and parental expectations for the school experience must be carefully reviewed. Parents and community values must be analyzed as you prepare the portfolio structure. For portfolios to be effective, the goals and instructional objectives of the schools must be identified as you develop a model.

The following models have been quite helpful in initial start-up activities, and as teachers' experience with portfolios grows, the models can be modified to accommodate new situations. The portfolio models are defined as a content outline for illustration, and several are presented.

---

**MODEL 1:** *Urbana City/Fairborn City, Grade 1 Portfolio, Fairborn, Ohio*

I.   Introduction

II.  The four content areas

   A.  Self-esteem

   B.  Academics—language arts concentration

   C.  Social skills

   D.  Work study skills

III. Guidelines to implementation

   A.  Storage

   B.  Grading: good, satisfactory, unsatisfactory

   C.  Cost

   D.  Checklists

Developed by Cynthia Jackson, Urbana City schools, and Barbara Wingard and Diane Eilers, Fairborn City Schools, June 1993; participants in a Portfolio Institute, Wright State University, June 1993.

---

---

**MODEL 2:** *Schnell School, Grade 4 Portfolio, West Carrollton, Ohio*

|  |  | *Topic* |
|---|---|---|
| I. | Self-portrait: | Decision making |
| II. | Academic: | Language arts—journals, logs |
|  |  | Mathematics—hands-on manipulatives |
| III. | Assessment data: | Test scores |
|  |  | Teacher reflections |
|  |  | Coopersmith Self-Esteem Inventory |
|  |  | IOWA |
|  |  | Academic achievement |

Developed by Schnell School, fourth grade faculty, March 1992.

---

**MODEL 3:** *Multi-Grade-Level Portfolio for Snowhill School, Grades 3 & 4, Springfield, Ohio*

I.  Letter to grade level teachers (fourth grade)

II.  Cover sheets

    A. Sheets to slip into front cover of 3-ring notebook or have students design on their own

    B. Rectangle for spine (student's name will go on this)

    C. Dedication sheet (might want this to be last activity students do for this portfolio)

III.  Attendance section

    A. School calendar for perfect attendance and copies of attendance honor rolls can be kept here*

    B. Certificates for perfect attendance and copies of attendance honor rolls can be kept here*

IV.  Project evaluation form (for use by student, teacher, parent)**

V.  Section on self-esteem

    A. Interest and reflective inventories

*(continued)*

*Model 3* Continued

    B. Family activities

    C. All about me activities

       1. Feelings

       2. Goals

       3. Autobiographical

    D. All about friends activities

VI. Drug abuse prevention

    A. Inventory of knowledge (can be pre-, posttest)

    B. Making responsible decisions (model)

    C. Refusal skills (model)

    D. Other drug prevention activities

VII. Information for teachers

    A. Articles and additional activity ideas

    B. Your own activities and ideas

\* Need to have one of each of these (or similar project) before sending to next grade level.

\*\* Need to have four of these (or similar project) before sending to next grade level.

Developed by Joy Johnson, Jewel McDonald, Barb Mack, and Michael Weaver, June 1993.

---

**MODEL 4:** *Milton Union Elementary School, Grade 5 Portfolio, West Milton, Ohio*

I. Title page and table of contents

II. Who am I?

    A. Introduce self

    B. Family

    C. Friends

III. Success at school

    A. Attendance

    B. Behavior

    C. Goals

    D. Study skills

    E. Learning style

*(continued)*

*Model 4* Continued

    F.  Cooperative learning

IV.  Academic success

    A.  Reading

    B.  Writing

    C.  Science and health

    D.  Social studies

    E.  Math

    F.  Journal responses

    G.  Speaking and listening record

    H.  Special projects

    I.  Competency records

V.  Lookin' back an' movin' on—reflections on the past year.

Developed by faculty, Milton Union School, June 1993.

---

**MODEL 5:** *Multi-Grade-Level and Elementary,*
*Southwest Ohio Schools*

I.  Introduction

    A.  Title page (student designed)

    B.  Statement of purpose

    C.  Student reaction (September and June)

    D.  Waiver of confidentiality (including sign-out sheet
        for reviewers

II.  Who I am

    A.  Interest inventory

    B.  Thoughts about junior high (September and June)

    C.  Work habits (inventory, personal, social skills)

    D.  Decision-making skills (exercises to develop skills
        for dealing with anger, conflict resolution, refusal to
        participate in harmful activities)

    E.  Self-concept activities (Coopersmith Self-Esteem
        Inventory)

*(continued)*

*Model 5* Continued

III. Goal setting and review

    A. Academic

    B. Behavioral

    C. Attendance

    D. Extracurricular (social)

    E. Life goals

IV. Academic and reflections

    A. Language arts (predominant)

    B. Science (best lab reports, tests)

    C. Social studies (projects, travel itinerary, tests)

    D. Health/Quest (service learning projects)

    E. Math (projects, tests, placement tests, Mathcounts)

    F. Music (solo or ensemble contests, concert articles)

    G. Art (pictures of projects, evaluations, etc.)

Developed by Joan Schindler (Incarnation); Alvine Wilson, Mary Galdeen, Deborah Carey, Rae Ann Herman (West Carrollton Junior High School); and Cindy Hill (Weisenborn Institute), June 1993.

In Models 2, 3, 4, and 5, a variety of elementary school models are illustrated. Each model was developed by practicing teachers after study of portfolio theory through selected published literature. Careful analysis by the faculty in these schools permitted development of a portfolio model to meet unique school needs.

**MODEL 6:** *West Carrollton Junior High School Portfolio Model, West Carrollton, Ohio*

        *Topic*

Section A    Career awareness

Section B    Self-portrait

Section C    Academic (language arts, health)

Section D    Drug education (Quest)

Developed by seventh grade faculty, March 1992.

**MODEL 7:** *Senior English Class Portfolio Model*

Purpose: Self-evaluation of skills and growth in writing of reading/writing response patterns

I.   Writing

    A. Choice of three essays

       1. Literature response

       2. Personal essay

       3. Defense paper

       4. Cause-and-effect paper

       5. Comparison paper

       6. Classification paper

    B. Peer edit form for each paper

    C. One required research paper

    D. Reflection on research paper

    E. Choice of one essay test on literature (list)

    F. Reflections on why each paper and test was chosen

II.  Reading

    A. Reflections on any literature pieces (list)

    B. Reflections on why RDGs and response chosen

III. Summary

    A. Self-evaluation of writing progress

    B. Analysis of peer edit, suggestions taken/not taken with explanations

    C. Analysis of strengths/weaknesses in writing

    D. Evaluation RDG responses (themes/patterns)

IV.  Guidelines

    A. Cost:  minimal (folders/boxes)

    B. Storage:  closed cupboard

    C. Evaluation:  points for work in PF
                          points for evaluation of work included

    D. Administration:  copy to principal/supervisor

Developed by Mari Lou Moore, Carol Dean Jan Jacobs, David Roushy, June 1993, representing three southwestern Ohio Schools.

*MODEL 8:* *Lima City Schools, Grades 10–12 Alternative High School Model, Lima, Ohio*

I. Introduction

   A. Title page

   B. Pre-reflections on why and importance of doing daily journal

   C. Post-reflections on why and importance of doing daily journal

II. Student Portrait

   A. Attendance goal 90%

   B. Topics for daily log

   C. Rate attitude (104)
      (Manners, willingness to work, completes assignments on time)

III. Educational Plan

   A. Proficiency test, drug survey, and self-esteem test results

   B. Intake forms, test of achievement in basic skills (TABE) results

   C. Student goals

   D. Copies of exceptional work

IV. Career Plan

   A. Career and education plan (part of intake)

   B. Short-term and long-term goals

V. Conclusion

   A. Reflection—goals for infusion back into regular schedule classes

   B. Evaluate short-term goals

   C. Expectations for future

Developed by LIMA OWE faculty, November 1991.

In Models 6, 7, and 8, the ideas of selected teachers in a junior high school, a senior high English class, and an alternative high school are presented. Portfolios used with the secondary grades will need further research and development, and secondary-level teachers are the best people to revise teaching practices via studying and implementing portfolios.

## Portfolios in Practice

To supplement portfolio efforts in the classroom, alternatives to traditional assessment practices must be found. For some, portfolios represent new report cards and affect the way students are graded (Jongsung, 1989). One example is the shift to progress reports and additional parent-teacher-student conferences. In fact, the conferencing approach allows for in-depth discussion of growth in a selected academic area (see Resources B and C for sample conference forms). It is also possible to specify areas of growth and particular remedial needs for the student. However, in the future, it will be necessary to move beyond simplistic folders with randomly collected artifacts of learning. The future requires use of electronic portfolios and sophisticated approaches for data collection and analysis.

## Instructional Materials: A Format With Flexibility

Assembling a great deal of material from every student can create a huge amount of paper, folders, tapes, and other documentations of the students' work. How to best present this variety of material in a format that aids ease of access, portability, and presentation challenges both teacher and student. Creating an understandable, usable, and user-friendly format for the student and teacher is necessary (Murphy & Smith, 1990). With so many suppliers of office materials available to the consumer, there seems to be a number of possibilities. In working with portfolio practitioners, a few examples of school usage have appeared in the classroom. Certainly, portfolios can be found in various shapes, containers, sizes, folders, and binders. Keeping the work accessible to both teacher and student is a primary concern. Because of the volume of material stored in the process portfolio, it tends to be (and needs to be) large and flexible.

File folders become cumbersome with so much material in them, and losing things that slip out remains a problem. Many portfolio programs have used this type of folder because it offers space to print on both sides of the folder and, much like a doctor's office, keeps a running track record of the student. This folder is the least expensive. Storage in a file cabinet works well, and the cabinet does not take up much space.

Some teachers have used accordion-type folders with string ties. Although taking up a little bit more space than a simple file folder, this type lends itself to being divided, with individual file folders for each subject area. Displaying or even working with such a folder tends to create an expansion, or sometimes an explosion, of paper and projects because in order to access anything from the folder, almost everything needs to be taken out to analyze the contents, creating a potential mix-up situation. These types of folders also tend to swallow tapes, photos, and computer disks, making it difficult to keep everything sequentially organized. Storing, toting, and transporting large, overstuffed, accordion-type folders en masse likewise can be problematic. They create a stacking hazard without the use of a box or crate. They also are hard to store on shelves, in file cabinets, and over time.

Pocket folders and Duo-Tang™-type folders are a cross between products that offer the accessibility of a folder with the permanence of a three-ring binder. There is a limit to the amount of material that will fit and a lack of display presentation space with the pockets. Of course, slippage from the pockets is a reality everyone has faced, the classic "it must have fallen out of my folder" excuse. Cost advantages, however, are obvious.

The three-ring binder presents the best in terms of format and flexibility. Using dividers and other three-ring inserts, one can create a versatile and usable portfolio. This also allows the student and teacher to pull pieces for the product portfolio, which can be a smaller three-ring binder portfolio. The three-ring binder, more than any other method, gives a finished appearance to everything that is placed within it. This is a clean approach with consistency that also gives the student opportunity for endless creativity. The student can create covers to be inserted, dividers, tabs, and a multitude of presentation approaches. Each student in the class can have an individualized portfolio with a somewhat standardized format for the class. Using binders also creates easy storage possibilities. Commercial shelves can be used for long-term storage. Price flexibility is a plus. A school could purchase binders in bulk and have them printed with the school logo; they also can be sold in the school bookstore for easy accessibility for all students. Students can insert hand- or typewritten pages, photo pages, audio-cassette and videocassette tray pages, or anything else that presents and displays their work. The possibility of endless, easy, understandable variations creates educational freedom and potential for both teacher and student. Plus, the sliding-cost factor can make this type of portfolio available at all economic levels.

## Summary

In this chapter, we have presented a rationale for portfolio use in assessing student academic work over selected periods of time. A number of schematic portfolio outlines were illustrated for use in K-12 school classrooms.

# 4

# The Professional Educator's Portfolio

---

*Objectives*

After studying this chapter, you should be able to

1. Develop and implement a professional teaching portfolio
2. Develop a colleague-review strategy for your portfolio

---

## Introduction

Concurrent with the development of student portfolios, educators should consider engaging in the professional portfolio process for self-development as evolving professional educators. The need for continual growth and development for teachers is imperative. In a learning society, educators need to document their personal effectiveness and grasp of new knowledge. A professional educator's portfolio offers a promising solution for documentation of teaching effectiveness and professional growth (Seldin, 1991). In this way, tangible and concrete evidence can be provided to administrators responsible for staff evaluation. Portfolios also provide a personal sense of accomplishment and individual growth. Important for professional self-assessment, educators must seek new avenues for professional enrichment and teaching improvement.

Professionals in such fields as architecture, art, and engineering have constructed portfolios to document expertise. As with the learning process, teaching is multidimensional and requires authentic assessment to accurately captivate the rich process of instructing. A teaching portfolio, carefully constructed, provides for varied documentation. Portfolios bring a variety of feedback sources on course design and performance into a meaningful configuration. A teaching portfolio serves as a communication tool for identifying teaching accomplishments. Thus portfolios serve as a communication tool permitting educators to mold the document around accomplishments.

Two purposes for the construction of portfolios by educators are as follows.

*1. To Identify Professional Growth.* The developing portfolio clarifies for the developers answers to such questions as

- Where am I professionally?
- Where have I been?
- Where am I going?

As Min Hong (1994), a New York City public schoolteacher explains,

> Even though I teach first grade every year, every year is different. So my portfolio helps me see how I'm evolving as a teacher. It helps me see where I've been, where I am, and—because I set goals—where I'm headed. I ask my students to keep portfolios, too, so I live the life I teach. (p. 50)

The professional takes ownership of his or her career path and designs the future course. This type of professional portfolio is usually more informal, selective, time limited, and self-reflective.

*2. For Personnel Decisions.* When portfolios are constructed for personnel considerations, caution must be taken to promote edu-

ownership. Portfolios place the initiative for documenting and displaying teaching back in the hands of the person who is doing it: "They put the teacher back in charge . . . selecting, assembling and explaining portfolio entries that accurately represent actual performance" (Seldin, 1991, p. 14). The intrinsic reward of constructing portfolios must be pursued. Thus portfolio construction for personnel use is usually more formal and comprehensive.

## Professional Portfolio Guidelines

In preparing a professional teaching portfolio, content inclusion must be considered. A professional educator portfolio incorporates a written description of a teacher's major strengths, teaching achievements, professional development activities, and professional career goals. Its primary purpose is to provide

1. Evidence of teaching effectiveness (student and peer reports, syllabi)
2. A structure for reflection on self-growth plans
3. Evidence of professional growth during one's career

Portfolios do not provide all evidence of teaching efforts, but selective quality data about serious efforts to improve performance and foster student learning are presented.

Therefore, the purpose for doing the portfolio must be first clarified. The teacher needs to consider who will read the portfolio and for what purposes they will read it. A portfolio constructed for oneself will remain basically in the author's domain, whereas a portfolio developed for personnel review will be read and digested by others, which calls for clarity. After establishing the purpose, identifying strengths to be highlighted within the portfolio should follow. Focus on positive teacher behaviors, characteristics, and accomplishments. The materials need to be arranged in a professional manner and constructed so the reader can progress through them easily. Large quantities of information can be arranged graphically (e.g., grades, evaluations from students). When multitudes of similar materials are significant, perhaps random sampling of items will suffice.

Several considerations should be reviewed before actual construction takes place. First, remember to include a description of your teaching philosophy and future goals. Decide how you will communicate to the reader about what you teach, why you teach in that manner, and the values of the actions to student learning. Information must come from a variety of sources: oneself, other professionals, and students. A description of how students apply learning and how the learning is assessed must be included. A table of contents or index must be placed early in the portfolio for usability. Page numbers must be placed on each entry, and page number identification must appear on the index or table of contents.

---

### Suggested Items for Inclusion

1. Teaching philosophy or teaching beliefs
2. What you teach and why
3. How you teach and with what
4. Your effective teaching characteristics or behaviors
5. Student learning documentation from your teaching
6. Student application and evaluation of learning
7. Student and colleague acknowledgment of your teaching
8. Your professional development plan of action
9. Teaching goals
10. Methods used to improve teaching

---

Because portfolios should be updated regularly, it is strongly suggested that the author use a word processor. Word processing saves time and promotes a more favorable avenue for changes. Review the completed portfolio, checking for balance between artifacts from yourself, others, and products of good teaching that lead to learning. Before submitting the portfolio for review, permit another educator to assess it while responding to the following questions:

### Review Questions

1. What is my teaching philosophy and what are my future goals?
2. What do I teach and why?
3. What makes me an effective teacher?
4. What do my colleagues, students, and I say about my teaching?
5. What strategies do I use in teaching? What materials do I use?
6. How do you know students apply learning in my class?
7. In what ways do students apply learning in my class?
8. How do you know that I am a developing professional and problem solver?

After completing the review, if your colleague answers these questions satisfactorily, you can assume your documentation accurately portrays your teaching. If the reviewer fails to respond to any question, you should improve the communication of data involved in the problematic area.

The following model presents content for inclusion in the portfolio.

### A Professional Portfolio Model

| Content | Entry Items |
|---|---|
| Personal material | Current teaching responsibilities |
| | Teaching philosophy |
| | Teaching goals for the next 5 years |
| | Sample syllabi |
| | Self-improvement evidence |
| | Sample curricular revisions |

| Material from others | Peer evaluations |
| --- | --- |
| | Administrator evaluations |
| | Student evaluation data |
| | Teaching recognitions |
| | Evidence of advanced training in teaching |
| Teaching products | Student creative work |
| | Evidence of impact on students |
| | Alumni comments |
| | Teacher-graded materials |

Guard against considering the professional educator portfolio as an instrument for performance appraisal only. It can represent teaching effectiveness and growth as well as professional activities, and it connects evidence from a range of professionals regarding growth as a teacher.

## The Career Portfolio

The professional portfolio is presented as a process for developing career objectives, assisting with career decisions, and adding a developmental perspective to the work of teaching. The portfolio can provide a window on interests, satisfactions, and needs to assist us in revitalizing a career that may have lost its appeal. It is appropriate to reflect on the meaning of teaching and whether one is personally growing. Loss of interest leads one to plod through the motions of teaching without real zest for the learning environment. School environments provide a rich and changing scene in which to work with an ever-shifting array of personalities in the age group of 5 to 18. Teachers are helpers who like to work with people—to inform, enlighten, help, train, develop, or cure them (Holland, 1973). As a professional in this career field, it is vital to continually examine the kinds of people with whom you prefer to spend time, the kinds of activities you enjoy doing, and how your personal interests are being met.

Portfolios will provide a broad and in-depth picture of a person's growth and development and have the potential for providing career direction that is stronger and more effective than traditional career counseling. The portfolio assists the teacher and administrator in molding reflective thoughts regarding values, family issues, career needs, and career planning. It provides an opportunity to analyze needs in a broader context, the context of life as it relates to career goals for the future. Few adults have the luxury to pause and place in perspective the impact of career on self-concept and life roles. A portfolio provides a direct intervention that helps individuals face the need to reflect on career plans for the future.

A portfolio provides documented information about the following career issues:

- Analysis of teaching goals
- Analysis of administration goals
- Evidence of professional effectiveness in teaching and administration
- Records of changes resulting from self-evaluation
- Evidence of participation in professional development seminars
- Professional evaluations by others
- Plans for the future

The portfolios permit teachers and administrators to blend past learning experiences with current goals and career aspirations. Also, leadership skills in organization, analysis, professional judgment, and educational values are documented. In sum, both teacher and administrator will benefit from a systematic review of their professional work and future plans.

The following model is recommended for use by professional educators.

| A Professional Portfolio | | |
|---|---|---|
| | *Content Area* | *Suggested Content* |
| I. | Introduction | What this portfolio is about |
| II. | Self-analysis | Self-evaluative data |
| | | Psychological profile |
| | | Self-reports |
| III. | Teaching | Teaching responsibilities |
| | | Teaching philosophy |
| | | Teaching goals for next 5 years |
| | | Teaching syllabi |
| | | Self-evaluation steps |
| IV. | Career plans | Resumé |
| | | Career experiences the past 10 years |
| | | Professional goals for next 5 years |
| | | Educational training plans |

In constructing your portfolio, a 2-inch, three-ring binder or an executive-style leather binder with plastic sleeves is recommended. Placing your name in bold letters on the cover or spine of the portfolio makes identification quick and easy. The portfolio must be neatly assembled and well organized.

Teaching accomplishments must be documented in the portfolio. Evidence should be required from three sources: teaching evidence, personal evidence, and collegial evidence.

**Examples of Teaching Evidence**

- Student learning examples (class projects, work samples, etc.)
- Individual student projects
- Formal evaluation results, supporting teaching
- Higher level thinking skill results (problem-solving activities)

**Examples of Personal Evidence**

- Planning: lessons and units
- Specific student pedagogy
- Classroom organization and management policies
- Professional growth information
- Cultural diversity instruction
- Technology updating

**Examples of Collegial and Student Evidence**

- Formal and informal document of effective teaching from other educators
- Student assessment results
- Awards and honors
- Videotaping with peer analysis

By providing evidence from these categories, clarity and accuracy result. This, in turn, enables school administrators to make better personnel decisions and professionals to better assess their individual development.

In summary, the professional educator's portfolio should include a statement of desires, accomplishments, and plans for the future, as well as a description of major strengths and plans for remediating areas of weakness. A professional portfolio provides a sense of accomplishment and achievement in the field of education. A portfolio provides the structure for self-reflection about which areas of teaching performance need improvement (Pascal & Wilburn, 1978).

---

### *Professional Portfolio Considerations*

- When teaching portfolios are used, the reward system becomes more responsive to teaching.
- Portfolios can be infused into current evaluation practices with limited disruption.
- Teaching portfolios are both process and product oriented. By constructing the portfolio, the instructor makes instructional decisions that enhance teaching performance.

- For best results, portfolios should be individualized and comprehensive.
- Selectivity must be used. Portfolios are not a total compilation of documents and materials.
- Manageability, cost, and time efficiency must be addressed in designing portfolios.
- Guidelines must be given to educators if they are to construct portfolios for personnel decisions.
- Assertions identified in the portfolio must have empirical evidence for support.
- For portfolios to have the maximum impact for the constructors, they should be shared with others and responses obtained from the individuals reading them. Feedback helps in clarifying improvement strategies.

## Portfolios for Administrators

Whereas the above content has focused on the professional teacher's portfolio, public school administrators should likewise consider initiating portfolios of their professional growth that would document learning acquired through theoretical and practical experiences. A portfolio would be an exercise in self-evaluation, introspection, analysis, and synthesis. The administrator should relate past learning experiences through his or her educational and administrative goals to exhibit critical self-analysis and to demonstrate the ability to organize documentation in a clear, concise manner. The experience of developing a portfolio will allow the administrator to extend his or her self-esteem as an administrator and enhance his or her ability to clarify and reach life and work goals. In addition, the portfolio serves as an excellent record of effectiveness in work situations, suitable for presentation to board of education members for review and to others interested in the administrator's skills on the job.

As a vehicle for developing administrative reflectivity, the portfolio provides a means of analyzing, synthesizing, and integrating
a variety of knowledge as well as a means of both training and
gaining practical experience. Documentation of the following
should be included in the portfolio.

---

***Administrative Documentation***

1. Professional career goals
2. Professional growth plan
3. Professional evidence of competence in administration

---

We suggest that the following content areas be considered by the
administrator for inclusion in his or her portfolio. A number of
sources have documented anywhere from 10 to 12 skill areas in
which a practicing school administrator must demonstrate competence and skill. These include curriculum development, staff su-
pervision, staff development, public relations, school finance,
school law, computer management, staff personnel assessment,
school business management, and perceptiveness in dealing with
the staff and school board.

A professional portfolio will permit documentation of skill and
competence in the above areas through formal courses, seminars,
workshops, self-study, and practical, on-the-job experience. Suggested evidence of administrator competence includes national examinations completed and passed, formal course work completed,
independent study and research, professional conferences, and
workshops attended and certificates held. In addition, a variety of
other professional experiences—acquired from teaching and administration via sample reports, plans, and data analysis—can be
included in the portfolio. We also suggest that the portfolio include
a resumé and statement of philosophy. Administrators should
demonstrate the ability to reflect on the critical issues facing learning in the schools and the problems in organizing and managing
schools. Administrators must remember that the portfolio is not a

scrapbook but a carefully constructed set of evidence that demonstrates administrator competence in a number of key areas, including the ability to reflect and solve critical educational problems. When constructing the portfolios, administrators must pause and reflect on the meaning of their work and how they are dealing with the multitude of issues that affect student learning, including managing of schools, budgeting for schools, and demonstrating accountability to the public.

## Summary

In this chapter, the theory of portfolio use was reviewed and a process for professional educators outlined. A career portfolio is essential for documenting professional growth and assisting teachers in maintaining a zest for teaching as a career. We believe the potential for continual self-growth will be enhanced through the development of a professional portfolio.

# Technology and Portfolios in the Future

Bonnie K. Mathies

---

### *Objectives*

After studying this chapter, you should be able to

1. Explain both the potential and power of technology in the classroom via portfolios

2. Identify a number of computer technologies for classroom use

3. Discuss the current evolution of instructional materials and describe their influence on the future of high-tech portfolios of the future

4. Identify various case studies of successful school use of combining technology and portfolios

---

## Introduction

Teachers can no longer play the role of authority and dispenser of knowledge. Interdisciplinary and learning-outcomes-oriented curricula require more collaborative work and team teaching. There is a need for authentic assessment of real problems and real tasks dealt with by students. Portfolio implementation and development permits learners to take more responsibility for managing their own learning. Students build on their out-of-school as well as in-school interests, experiences, and knowledge. Using the world as their resource rather than just the teacher, students begin to navigate their own lifelong voyage of self-directed learning. Using technologies currently available, teachers have the opportunity to set up a learning environment that will enable students to build a ship that can sail the seas of lifelong learning using portfolios as both a map and a compass.

> Teachers are seeking ways of setting up learning environments that are more realistic than traditional classrooms. There are many reasons for this emphasis, including the need to help students become better problem solvers. Computers and related technology can be used to help create realistic problem-solving situations, as well as providing tools to help pose and solve problems. (Kearsley, Hunter, & Furlong, 1992, p. 3)

Releasing the power of technology in the classroom via portfolios will enable the teacher to reach more students effectively and efficiently while engaging the students in a more meaningful process of learning.

The microcomputer established itself in the U.S. classroom during the mid-1980s, and since that time, educators have been searching for strategies and techniques to integrate computer-based technology into the schoolhouse. Educators discovered early on that computers could potentially increase their productivity through the use of word processing, database programs, spreadsheets, and graphics capabilities. With this technology, the school and the classroom could be more efficient with more time available for student-centered interactions. Computers, when used correctly, reduce the time spent on the tasks that teachers perform on a daily basis: keeping grades and taking attendance, creating and scoring tests, writing letters to parents, and keeping records of all kinds. However, the power of technology has the ability to go beyond simply increasing classroom management efficiency and teacher productivity. Using technology via portfolios in the classroom integrates a learning environment that has the potential for creating a more realistic and educationally beneficial adventure for both the student and teacher.

Schools have a relatively short history of using computer-based technology. Most of the technology used has been isolated and primarily noninteractive. If anything, most computers in education are used as expensive typewriters and fancy dictionaries or encyclopedias. The biggest part of collaborative student learning in the classroom has been limited to fighting over who will get to use the computer next. Typically, schools have had single, stand-alone computers not connected to any kind of network; computer labs have been established rather than scattering computer stations throughout classrooms; and multimedia tools have supported only lecture-type activities by the teacher as opposed to individual student research, exploration, or production. Even telecommunications has been difficult to implement because classrooms usually do not have telephones, and district policies or systems do not allow for easy access to the few that do exist in a school. The adventure of learning with technology has been a nightmare for many administrators, teachers, and students, many times an expensive nightmare.

## The Power of Technology in the Classroom

During the mid-1980s, the initial exploration as well as discovery of the once-uncharted territory of technology emerged. Currently, this exploring stage has evolved into a developmental stage.

More and more classrooms are being networked together with other classrooms, other schools, other communities, and even other countries. Fiber-optic networks, cable in the classroom, and satellite broadcast informational systems are all becoming readily available. Hardware prices have plummeted, and the ability to up-grade systems has vastly improved. New software now encour-ages critical thinking, decision making, and development of materials. Assessment of student progress is changing, with the focus now more on the process of learning through oral and writ-ten communication and less on student performance with paper-and-pencil tests (Kearsley et al., 1992).

The market penetration of computer-based technology in schools reached amazing levels during 1994. According to *Market Data Retrieval* (Holt, 1994), an intensified interest in educational technology in K-12 schools has occurred, with the ratio of micro-computers to students continuing to decrease to a 1:9.6 national average. Since 1991, there has been astonishing growth in CD-ROMs, local area networks, and videodiscs. Growth forces causing this change include increased (though still sporadic) funding, con-cern about equal access or equity issues, recognition of the neces-sity of technology literacy skills, the "un-textbook" classroom environment, and the growth of interdisciplinary curricula.

The power of educational technology resides in its ability to teach. Educators have begun using small cooperative learning groups to solve problems. Electronic telecommunications net-works extend beyond the walls of the classroom to include world resources. Ideas can be presented to entire classes using projection tools like LCD panels. Customized individual student goals and learning styles can be accommodated with the unleashed flexibil-ity that technology offers both the student and the teacher.

## Technology in the Classroom

The past 10 years have seen amazing changes in the type, role, and function of instructional materials. The infusion of a variety of technology into the classroom has allowed educators the freedom to experiment with innovative teaching and assessment strategies. Students are now able to construct new knowledge rather than just be passive receivers of knowledge. Computer-based technology has permitted students to assume responsibility for managing their own learning. Previous materials were text based and linear, whereas new technologies include still and moving images that jump from segment to segment based on user interest and need. Bringing the learning process alive and using the portfolio to document the products of this process requires various technologies. Today, a great deal of technology is available in many forms, and when first exploring this technology, the terminology can be daunting. The following terms are common and should be mastered by users of this material:

*Modems.* Modems, used to connect computers to a remote network using a telephone line, convert the computer information (which is digital data) into a form that can be accepted by the telephone (which requires analog data). The time will come when the telephone systems we use will be digital and modems will be unnecessary.

*LANs and WANs.* Local area networks (LANs) and wide area networks (WANs) are growing in scope and usefulness. A LAN or WAN connects computers together without the use of telecommunications hardware. The computers are wired together, and a number of configurations are possible. A LAN might be within a classroom or throughout an entire building. A WAN usually encompasses a larger area, such an entire school district, and could include community entities such as libraries, museums, and hospitals.

*Servers.* Servers come in many sizes and complexities. Basically, they are dedicated computers that manage networks. Servers often house data and permit the sharing of resources such as printers. Integrated learning systems use servers to manage instruction, and many cooperative efforts can be supported by servers facilitating work groups that need to share data and collaborate with each other.

*School networks.* Using this technology, some of the first school networks typically have been used for transferring and sharing administrative data, such as test results, grades, attendance, and reports. Newer software has given educators desktop capability to enter grades, analyze progress, and send personalized letters to parents. Teachers with modems and computers at home are now also able to access student information or curricular databases at any time.

*On-line databases.* Information retrieval from on-line databases is growing in popularity as the ease and comfort of going to the library at any time of day via your home or work computer increases. Access is sometimes limited to membership or enrollments such as an America Online account or student status at a university. Free Nets provide community access to local information and libraries. Local electronic bulletin boards and commercial providers to global networks like the Internet have opened communication doorways. There are many obstacles to be overcome in using telecommunications in schools, but the value of accessing information at any time and from any place and the ability to communicate with other educators and students around the world is hard to deny.

*Global educational networks.* Telecommunications hardware, such as a modem, computer, and some type of communications software, will link educators into a global educational network community. There are already networks specifically designed to link teachers and schools together. Learning Link, sponsored by the Public Broadcasting Service, is one such network. Forums on various topics, projects, and issues are available for both teachers and students. Commercial networks, such as CompuServe, Prodigy, America Online, and Scholastic Network, have also begun to include menu opportunities for learning, teaching, and research.

*Optical media.* This term currently refers to laser discs and CD-ROMs. The advantage of optical media is random access. This means that unlike a videocassette or an audiotape, the user simply moves to any image or moving sequence instantly, and the time spent moving back and forth on a tape is eliminated. Optical media are made of plastic and coated with a shiny, durable finish designed to reflect light from a laser beam. The beam reads the information embedded in pits on the surface of the disc. When the laser beam strikes one of these pits, the light is reflected to a mirror and then onto a decoder in the player. The disc then converts this reflected light into audio, video, or command code, depending on data originally stored on the master (Floyd, 1991).

*Laser discs.* Laser discs appear to be a cross between a 12-inch phonograph album and an audio CD. One side of a videodisc can contain 54,000 numbered images or frames, and they can be frozen in place to show a still picture or can play the images continuously to show moving footage.

*CD-ROM.* CD-ROM, which stands for compact disk-read only memory, is familiar in size to most people because music compact disks have been around for a few years. A CD-ROM can hold approximately 400 high-density, 3.5-inch disks of information, or more than 180,000 pages, all on one side. CD-ROMs now can also contain words, images, graphics, and sound. The equipment needed to play a video disc is a laser disc player, and likewise, CDs are played on either internal or external CD players.

*Photo CDs.* Photo CD capabilities offer an exciting first step to supplement a traditional portfolio. The program *Kodak Create-It* provides tools to design an interactive photo portfolio. Images, text charts, and audio files can be imported easily. *Kodak Arrange-It CD Portfolio Layout Software* enables the user to systematically lay out sophisticated multimedia programs. Electronic books, displays, and presentations can be created.

*Multimedia.* Multimedia are just that—a combination of a variety of formats, such as still and moving images, sound, text, and graphics. The cost of multimedia-supportive equipment and multimedia development tools has decreased so that teachers and students can reasonably afford the capability to produce multimedia materials such as portfolios. The combination of various media formats permits students to learn more spontaneously and more naturally, using whatever sensory modes they prefer. Student experiences can be captured, documented, and shared via multimedia portfolios. Students take an active role in their learning as the development of the electronic portfolio proceeds.

Multimedia portfolios can add an important complement to the total assessment of the learner. Given the currently converging standards of optical and digital media, the opportunity exists to infuse the process of integrated, individualized curriculum development with collective portfolio evaluation efforts. Using the technology of today, we have the potential of reaching the educational goals of tomorrow for students, teachers, administrators, school systems, communities, and beyond. However, maintaining an extremely personalized portfolio and actively staying in touch with students will require teachers, parents, and administrators to practice conferencing on a regular basis.

## High-Tech Portfolios With High-Tech Assessment

Assessment of learning activities while using all of this technology can become more difficult and complex. However, as the use of computer-based technologies and information retrieval systems becomes more integrated and readily available, use by teachers as well as students will become easier. When the automobile was first developed, most horse riders used the same excuse, that driving a car was more difficult and complex. Yet as more and more people began driving instead of riding, the automobile became a way of life, seamlessly integrated into the fabric of society. Technology is experiencing the same phenomenon in education.

Skills that students are now being asked to demonstrate more and more in today's world include gathering, organizing, and sharing information; analyzing relationships; testing hypotheses; and communicating the results effectively and efficiently. Traditional testing techniques no longer provide a clear evaluation of these desired learning outcomes. Computer-assisted portfolio assessment provides a more appropriate and adaptable model of student assessment. Portfolio software systems such as the *Grady Profile* help teachers organize the multitude of data accumulated about their students. The *Grady Profile* provides insights and highlights students' strengths and needs, and one of its features is the student profile. The student profile contains many aspects of students that relate to their capabilities, scholastic performance, and personal growth, such as family information, medical data, behavior at schools, standardized test results, reading and writing capabilities, math skills, and so on. Each student has a hypercard stack that provides information pertinent to his or her identity. Some features that each card can provide include writing samples, video samples, teacher remarks, oral reading samples, penmanship, and cross-curriculum outcomes and team projects (Grady, 1992).

Although the majority of portfolios today tend to be mostly text based (student writing), the addition of videotape clips, audiotapes, still photographs, and artifacts expand and clarify portfolio development. The immediate concern is usually how to manage the mechanics of storing such varied types of media. Now, with the presently converging digital standard of optical media and desktop multimedia revolution, this concern will soon be a moot point. Everything from writing samples, video clips, audiotapes, still photographs, and artifacts to evaluation comments, progress notes, conference summaries, and anything else in a student portfolio will fit on one compact disc. It is currently somewhat expensive and complex to develop CD-ROMs in most schools; however, the capability and cost is rapidly becoming feasible, and within a short time, students will be able to archive their portfolio materials on a CD-ROM and press inexpensive copies for family and friends as well as job and college interviews.

It is currently possible and reasonably affordable to supplement the traditional text-based portfolio with a second collection placed on a videocassette or a videotaped multimedia presentation. A camcorder video camera will permit convenient taping of events, artifacts, computer text, and graphical documents. Simple editing decks will allow for adding in clips of student performances or presentations, and character generators provide a means to add words as well as graphics to video segments. Voice-over sound capabilities can even allow the addition of descriptive and reflective statements by the student producer or teacher.

Teachers are now creating portfolios of their teaching performance and are allowing these professionally intimate portraits to be used in their annual performance evaluations. An issue that certainly should be considered for both the teacher and the student is access and training in using video equipment, especially video editing equipment. Although the task of editing is not difficult, it does take some minor orientation to the equipment, and access should be available before school, after school, and on the weekends.

Regardless of which technological format you choose, whether multimedia CD-ROM based or camcorder-enhanced video, placing portfolios in an electronic format is challenging and requires more time at first. But as the learning curve accelerates and both the teacher and student begin to develop and exploit the potential and power of technology, they will soon see that the results are worth the effort as another evaluation dimension is provided.

## The Evolution of Instructional Materials

As this entire complex maze of various technology media and formats continues to unravel, the evolution of instructional materials explodes every day. An inverted pyramid of current applications demonstrates that there is a large base of word processing users that has already moved into desktop publishing. Soon, if not already, these desktop publishers will become presentation-authoring designers and multimedia developers. This sets the stage for hypermedia applications, such as *LinkWay, HyperCard,* and *HyperStudio.* Presentation software, such as *PowerPoint, Astound,* and *Persuasion,* and authoring programs, such as *Authorware, Icon Author,* and *Ten-CORE,* facilitate the design, development, delivery, and management of mediated presentations and computer-based instructional programs.

## Classroom Uses: Examples of Use in Speech, Music, Art, and Science

Clearly, all of this integration of technology in the classroom has tremendous potential as an educational tool. The ABC News interactive program *The Great Quake of '89* takes you to the night when the earth shook in San Francisco, and it brims with footage of burning buildings, news reports as the night and ensuing days progressed, and impassioned interviews with rescuers and victims.

Warner New Media's Audio Notes package *The Magic Flute* presents Mozart's opera, allowing students to view a measure-by-measure commentary on the music. Students can listen and learn about music in a new way.

*Draw and Color Funny Doodles With Uncle Fred* is a K-6 videodisc program incorporating math, language, social studies, science, music, social skills, and art. *Uncle Fred* uses active listening skills and visual aids, and it requires student participation. Students enhance motor skills as they use hand-eye coordination and learn to follow oral and visual instruction.

National Geographic has produced a comprehensive videodisc journey through 200 years of American history with a special emphasis on geography in *GTV: A Geographic Perspective on American History*. The program features 40 video clips, 1,600 still images, and 200 maps illustrating the American experience from pre-Columbian days to the present.

The American Association of Physics Teachers has produced a videodisc set called *Physics: Cinema Classics*, which presents more than 250 demonstrations of physics principles. The collection was designed to support teachers who wanted to motivate the visual learner. The set contains over 2,000 video segments and still images, accompanied by an instructor's hints, as well as two separate audio channels that contain discussion questions, explanations, and more.

Foreign language learning has been enhanced by the application of interactive videodiscs and CD-ROMs. Photographs and video sequences are included in the instruction as well as recorded audio. Optical media often have more than one audio track available, with one in English and others in a foreign language such as Spanish or

Japanese. Clips from these programs could be used with student translations to demonstrate language acquisition. Interactive science labs and many other cross-curricular considerations can be tied together with portfolios.

Instructional materials in the form of videodiscs and CD-ROMs have special relevance to the arts as media that can convey visual images, motion, and sound simultaneously. Art and music teachers have discovered the excitement that these media can convey. Student portfolios could contain a student's selection of favorite art works or music accompanied with reflections on why the choices were made.

## School Support Culture: Impact of Technology

The Georgia Statewide Academic and Medical System (GSAMS) is the world's largest and most comprehensive distance learning and health care network. Led by Governor Zell Miller, this groundbreaking public-private partnership is a trailblazing initiative that is changing the course of education and the delivery of health care in Georgia. By networking students and teachers with doctors and patients, GSAMS challenges children from all over Georgia to explore new educational frontiers and makes state-of-the-art medical care available in every corner of the state. With the help of telephone lines, video cameras, and television monitors, GSAMS links K-12 public schools, colleges, universities, adult and technical schools, hospitals, prisons, Georgia's Public Television Network, and even Zoo Atlanta together in a fully interactive, two-way environment (Allen & Rogers, 1994). Students involved in GSAMS programs could extract examples of interviews with students from other parts of Georgia who might work with them on a statewide group project, video observations from field experiences, or collections of research on topics of interest. These elements would enrich a student's portfolio.

Five Points Elementary School, Fairborn City Schools, is Ohio's largest elementary school, with approximately 1,500 students. In spite of financial difficulties, Fairborn City Schools has made a commitment toward technology infusion throughout the school district. Although most of the technology support has come from an active PTO and involvement with business partners, the district has also reallocated resources based on this recognized technology priority. Five Points has 121 computers and 1,475 students, with a ratio of one computer for every 12 students. The district plans to lower this ratio. There are two dedicated math instruction labs of 32 and 36 Macintosh computers with CD players and printers, and three Macintosh minilabs in Chapter 1 classrooms. The Information Technology Center, formerly the library media center, houses a large collection of optical media (125+ CDs and 100+ laser discs) along with a typical print collection. A portion of the center is devoted to a technology lab. All K-6 students visit the center at least one period per week. If schedule time permits, there are open times in the center schedule for students to do research and exploration. Students and teachers can use the technology lab when other classes are in the center.

Christopher Columbus School in Union City, New Jersey, and Bell Atlantic have worked together to connect schools and homes with computers and high-speed networks. The project involves a population of 135 children and 20 teachers and administrators. Each participant has a 486, 33 MHz PC at home, and there are 40 computers spread throughout the school. Union City has the highest minority population of any school district in New Jersey and is the most densely populated locality in the United States. The Union City School District is in the midst of a massive curriculum restructuring effort and is moving toward a whole language approach. The first phase of the project has demonstrated that technology has been successfully integrated as a tool to accomplish the goals of the curriculum, it has had a positive impact on writing, and there is continued growth of thematic planning and interdisciplinary units. Teacher and student attendance improved, Early Warning Test Scores (EWT) rose, homework was turned in, and students demonstrated more interest in classroom activities (Grady, 1994).

## Technology in the Future

Educational technology helps motivate students to learn by making learning more fun, giving them greater understanding in context, and enabling them to take a more active role in their learning. Teachers are finding that students enjoy learning how to use technology for many reasons:

- Learning is self-paced.
- Access to information is easy.
- Learning becomes more fun.
- Learning is independent and discovery-oriented.

This combination of elements enables students to learn more spontaneously and more naturally, using whatever sensory modes they prefer. Combining media elements with well-designed interactive exercises means that students are able to extend their experience, to discover on their own so that they are no longer sitting passively while information is fed to them. By taking an active part in their learning and using their senses to experience new situations, they can begin and complete their assignments with a broader, more in-depth understanding (Floyd, 1991).

Market trends indicate a growing infusion of instructional technology in education. Nineteen of 22 states that are textbook adoption states have revised their definition of "textbook," and many have now included selected videodisc series as "textbooks." Hand-held information appliances similar to Apple's Newton are finding their way into the schoolhouse. Multimedia curricula are mushrooming along with massive numbers of multimedia materials. CD-ROM software sales to schools are passing videodisc sales. Software firms traditionally in the school market are now testing the home market. Internet fever rages on.

There are bottlenecks in K-12 schools to technology integration. The age and mix of technology in the schools is overwhelming and problem-ridden, most school buildings are not electronically able to incorporate technology, there is a low density of technology in schools, computers are in labs rather than classrooms, and there is a general lack of technical support for technology users. Currently, there seems to be a lack of consensus among boards of education and policymakers about what should be done about technology. Schools are attempting to make the transition to knowledge acquisition and mentoring, yet there are poor models for integration into the curriculum and weak staff development programs. Industry is

responding to these problems by stepping up partnering opportunities and, in some cases, retrenching. Through the National Network for Educational Renewal, sixteen colleges of education are forming partnerships for school improvement, and a number of these sites have collaborated on the portfolio as a nontraditional assessment process for documenting student learning (Goodlad, 1990).

## Portfolios in the Future

Even though the current climate for schools' producing their own CDs is improving, educators should consider the eventuality of optical media, particularly in the creation of student or class portfolios. There are three basic steps to creating a CD-ROM product:

1. Recording the desired information (text, images, sound) in digital form and organizing how it is presented, along with software needed to use it [add narrative evaluations]
2. Setting up that information as it will appear on the CD, testing it to see if it will operate as you envisioned it, then creating an International Organization for Standards image
3. Premastering, mastering, and replicating the discs (Caffarelli & Straughan, 1992)

Other issues to be considered in the future spread and growth of educational technology via portfolios also can be attributed to the national focus on school restructuring and educational reform. Educators must keep in mind that computer-based technology and portfolios will not transform education; rather, schools must redesign and renew themselves to make the best use of the potential of portfolio technology. Schools should consider future development of their own optical media. Because the storage space on each disc is enormous and the product can be searched rapidly and electronically, CD-ROMs can be developed to disseminate archived materials such as mediated portfolios, portfolio support materials, and internal collections of written work. There are many applications of videodisc technology that would support the development of videodiscs in the schoolhouse. Because they are excellent storage mediums for quality video footage, footage of school events, productions, and student performances could be stored on one disc for a video yearbook. Videodiscs can add visual and audio realism to student and teacher portfolios.

Technology-based portfolios support individual, self-paced learning as well as large group instruction. The combination of pictures, text, and sound make laser discs, CD-ROMs, and other optical-based media more usable by people with different learning abilities or preferences. Some learners understand better by hearing or seeing than simply reading. Applications might include full-motion presentations of events such as a civil rights march, large collections of still images such as art collections, complete symphonies, or simulations of chemistry experiments. All of this and so much more can be possible simply by releasing the potential and power of technology in the classroom via portfolios.

A common barrier to the development of electronic portfolios is the need for initiating the early and constant collection of materials, such as videotaping events as well as activities for future editing; making audiocassette tapes of interviews; and collecting documents, photographs, and examples of support materials (Resource D provides a list of software publishers). The final 2 or 3 weeks of the school year are obviously not the time to begin gathering materials together to create a CD-ROM portfolio. It needs to be an ongoing process planned well in advance. The same problems exist for teacher portfolios. A need for prior planning and archiving materials in preparation for the final document must be considered.

## Summary

Both the process and products of evaluation need to change if education is to keep up with the changing world in which we live today. Interdisciplinary and learning-outcomes-oriented curricula require more collaborative work, team teaching, and authentic assessment methods. Using technology in the classroom via the portfolio can create a systematic and organized collection of evidence that both the student and teacher can use to monitor and develop knowledge, skills, and attitudes. Providing authentic and meaningful documentation of students' abilities is necessary. Portfolio implementation, when developed correctly, permits everyone involved more responsibility for managing and adapting the learning process. Releasing the power of technology in the classroom via portfolios will create a more effective, efficient, and realistically meaningful process of learning by tying together curriculum, instruction, and assessment.

# Resources

## Resource A

ISSUES IN PORTFOLIO DEVELOPMENT

*Portfolio Content:* Traditional assessment and instruction

*Teacher Concerns/Implementation*
- How can portfolios meld with report cards?
  - Supplement report cards with narratives.
- How can you accommodate for skills expectations?
  - Develop observational strategies for recording skills growth.

*Portfolio Content:* Organization

*Teacher Concerns/Implementation*
- How can you avoid "hit or miss" portfolios?
  - Proceed slowly with any changes.
  - Start with structure and use forms for observations.

- How can portfolios provide the most information about each learner?
  - Limit the number of samples selected.

*Portfolio Content:* Selection

*Teacher Concerns/Implementation*

- What materials should be selected for the portfolio?
  - Select samples that illustrate areas of strength and weakness.
- Who selects the materials?
  - Allow participation of student and parents in material selection.

*Portfolio Content:* Retention of materials

*Teacher Concerns/Implementation*

- How do you find a balance between what is sent home and what is kept?
  - Develop weekly folders to be sent home to parents.
- Do you pass the portfolio on to the next teacher?
  - Make copies of key pieces of the portfolio.
  - Retain selected samples from the beginning and end of the year for the next teacher.

*Portfolio Content:* Teacher's role

*Teacher Concerns/Implementation*

- How is a teacher's role in assessment different from the traditional classroom role?
  - Teachers become more aware of children and more active members of the classroom.

*Portfolio Content:* Student role

*Teacher Concerns/Implementation*

- What role do students have in the portfolio?
  - In selecting materials, students become more aware of their learning process.

*Portfolio Content:* Other school personnel

*Teacher Concerns/Implementation*

- How can portfolios be used in settings other than primary classrooms?
  - Develop content and select populations. Use notebooks or logs.
  - Use peer collaboration teams to evaluate and document progress.
- How do you maintain consistency and continuity with transient students?
  - Continue traditional report card use with supplemental portfolio documentation.
  - Maintain regular communication with caretakers to share evidence of progress.

## Resource B

### PORTFOLIO CONFERENCE REPORT

Subject/Class _____  Date _____

Teacher _____  Student _____

| *Portfolio* | | *Content Analysis* | |
|---|---|---|---|
| | Amount | Quality | Recommendations |

Subject area:

Subject area:

Subject area:

File

## Resource C

PORTFOLIO CONFERENCE SUMMARY

Subject/Class _____ Date _____

Teacher _____ Student _____

Conference Summary With Recommendations:

_____

_____

_____

_____

_____

_____

_____

_____

_____

_____

_____

_____

_____

_____

_____

_____

_____

_____

Student folder
Parents or guardian

# Resource D

## COMPUTER SOFTWARE RESOURCES

America Online, 8619 Westwood Center Dive, Vienna, VA 22182-2285, Ph. 800-727-6364.

*Astound*, Gold Disk, 3350 Scott Blvd., Santa Clara, CA 95954.

*Authorware*, Macromedia, 600 Townsend Street, San Francisco, CA 94103-4845, Ph. 415-252-2000.

CompuServ, 5000 Arlington Centre Blvd., Columbus, OH 43220, Ph. 800-848-8199.

*Draw and Color Funny Doodles With Uncle Fred*, Children's Bookstore, Ph. 800-455-5570.

*Grady Profile*, Aurbach & Associates, 130 Cremona Drive, Santa Barbara, CA 93116, Ph. 800-346-8355.

*GTV: A Geographic Perspective on American History*, National Geographic Society, 17th & M Streets NW, Washington, DC 20036, Ph. 800-368-2728.

*HyperCard*, Apple Corporation, 20525 Mariani Avenue, Cupertino, CA 95014, Ph. 408-996-1010.

*HyperStudio*, Apple Corporation, 20525 Mariani Avenue, Cupertino, CA 95014, Ph. 408-996-1010.

*Icon Author*, AIMtech Corporation.

*Kodak Photo CD Arrange-It*, 1187 Ridge Road W., Rochester, NY 14650-3011, Ph. 800-242-2424.

*Kodak Photo CD Create-It*, 1187 Ridge Road W., Rochester, NY 14650-3011, Ph. 800-242-2424.

*LinkWay*, IBM Corporation, 1133 Westchester Avenue, White Plains, NY 10601, Ph. 800-IBM-2468.

*Mozart's Magic Fantasy: The Magic Flute*, Children's Bookstore, Ph. 800-455-5570.

PBS Learning Link, 1320 Braddock Place, Alexandria, VA 22314-1698, Ph. 703-739-8464.

*Persuasion*, Aldus Corporation, 411 First Avenue S., Seattle, WA 98104-2870, Ph. 206-622-5000.

*Physics: Cinema Classics*, Children's Bookstore, Ph. 800-455-5570.

*PowerPoint*, Microsoft, One Microsoft Way, Redmond, WA 98052-6399, Ph. 800-227-4679.

Scholastic Network, P.O. Box 3720, Jefferson City, MO 65102-3720, Ph. 314-636-5271.

*TenCORE*, Computer Teaching Corporation.

*The Great Quake of '89*, ABC News, The Voyager Company, 1351 Pacific Coast Highway, Santa Monica, CA 90401, Ph. 213-451-1383.

# Annotated Bibliography
and References

## Annotated Bibliography

Adams, D. M., & Hamm, M. E. (1992). Portfolio assessment and social studies: Collecting, selecting, and reflecting on what is significant. *Social Education, 56*(2), 103-105.

*This article raises a number of important questions for teachers to consider as they develop a portfolio process (e.g., What type of physical container would hold representative pieces? How are portfolios evaluated? etc.).*

Batzle, J. (1992). *Portfolio assessment and evaluation: Developing and using portfolios in the K-6 classroom.* Cypress, CA: Creative Teaching.

*This workbook provides examples of how to organize, develop, and assess student portfolios; very good forms and checklists are presented.*

Belanoff, P., & Dickerson, M. (Eds.). (1991). *Portfolios: Process and product.* Portsmouth, NH: Boynton/Cook.

*A total of 23 articles comprise this excellent resource for evaluating student writing and establishing community standards for portfolio grading.*

Bernhardt, V. L. (1994). *The school portfolio*. Princeton, NJ: Eye Junction, Focus on Education.

*This book provides a framework for school improvement, criteria for assessment, and rules for quality planning. A leadership process is discussed with a focus on active community and parent partnerships.*

Bozzone, M. A. (1994, May/June). Professional portfolio: Why you should start one now. *Instructor*, pp. 47-50.

*This article captures the essence of developing a professional portfolio. Four teachers share the contents of their portfolios and the reasons portfolios are important to them as professionals.*

Camp, R. (1990). Thinking about portfolios. *The Quarterly of the National Writing Project and the Center for the Study of Writing, 12* (3), 8-14.

*The article provides a detailed description of the Arts PROPEL project and the PROPEL approach to portfolios. Its primary purpose is to create assessment closely integrated with institutions in the arts, such as visual arts, music, and imaginative writing.*

Fan, R., & Tone, B. (1994). *Portfolios and performances assessment.* New York: Harcourt Brace.

*Fan and Tone provide a strong review of authentic assessment through performance-based learning.*

Glanger, S. M., & Brown, C. S. (1993). *Portfolios and beyond: Collaborative assessment in reading and writing.* Norwood, MA: Christopher-Gordon.

*Chapters 1, 3, and 5 outline the framework for comprehensive assessment of the language arts program.*

Harp, B. (Ed.). (1993). *Assessment and evaluation in whole language programs.* Norwood, MA: Christopher-Gordon.

*Harp has edited an excellent review of assessment issues in whole language programs. Chapters 5 and 7 are particularly good on portfolio use.*

Jasmine, J. (1992). *Portfolio assessment for your whole language classroom.* Huntington Beach, CA: Teacher Created Materials, Inc.

*This monograph is designed to help the classroom teacher with portfolio assessment issues in the classroom (Grades 1-6). It provides step-by-step procedures for starting portfolios.*

Selden, P. (1991). *The teaching portfolio.* Bolton, MA: Anker.

> *Selden provides an excellent model for education and human service professionals who wish to develop their personal portfolios. A detailed list of items to include is presented.*

*Student Portfolios.* (1993). Washington, DC: National Education Association.

> *An excellent resource on school restructuring efforts, this small monograph focuses on portfolio assessment with an emphasis on longitudinal data gathering by students. Elementary and high schools are discussed, including a video portfolio model.*

Thomas, J. (1992, May). The new report cards: Portfolios are changing the way kids are getting graded. *Better Homes and Gardens,* pp. 34-36.

> *This article discusses "new" grading practices via actual school work to evaluate student progress. It also presents ideas to assist parents in starting a portfolio at home.*

Tierney, R. S., Carter, M. A., & Deseai, L. E. (1991). *Portfolio assessment in the reading-writing classroom.* Norwood, MA: Christopher-Gordon.

> *This is an excellent resource on portfolio use in the language arts area. A number of instructional strategies are illustrated.*

# References

Allen, M., & Rogers, W. (1994, September). *Georgia's instructional technology initiative.* Atlanta: Georgia Department of Education.

Caffarelli, F., & Straughan, D. (1992). *Publish yourself on CD-ROM: Mastering CDs for multimedia.* New York: Random House.

Carr, B. (1987). Portfolios. *School Arts, 86,* 55-56.

Cole, D. J., & Ryan, C. W. (1995, March). *Assessment of self-concept development through portfolios in a structured curriculum intervention process.* Paper presented at the annual meeting of the Eastern Education Research Association, Hilton Head, SC.

Dewey, J. (1904). The relation of theory to practice in the education of teachers. In *Third Yearbook of the National Society for the Study of Education—Part 1* (pp. 1-30). Bloomington, IL: Public School Publishing.

Farr, B., & Farr, R. (1990). *Language arts portfolio: Teachers manual.* New York: The Psychological Corporation and Harcourt, Brace, Jovanovich.

Flood, J., & Lapp, D. (1989). Reporting reading progress: A comparison portfolio for parents. *Reading Teacher, 42,* 508-514.

Floyd, S. (1991). *The IBM multimedia handbook: Complete guide to hardware and software applications.* New York: Brady.

Goodlad, J. (1990). *Teachers for our nation's schools.* San Francisco: Jossey-Bass.

Grady, E. (1992). *Grady Profile portfolio assessment: A performance-based assessment tool for teachers.* St. Louis, MO: Aurbach & Associates.

Grady, J. (1994). *Project Explore: A networked multimedia experience.* Union City, NJ: Bell Atlantic Video Services.

Hiebert, E. H., & Calfee, R. C. (1989). Advancing academic literacy through teachers' assessment. *Educational Leadership, 46*(7), 50-54.

Holland, J. (1973). *Making vocational choices: A theory of careers.* Englewood Cliffs, NJ: Prentice Hall.

Holt, J. (1994, September 21). EdNet'94 trends in educational technology. *Market Data Retrieval,* p. 9.

Jongsung, K. S. (1989). Portfolio assessment. *Reading Teacher, 43*(3), 264-265.

Kearsley, G., Hunter, B., & Furlong, M. (1992). *We teach with technology.* Wilsonville, OR: Franklin, Beedle & Associates.

Killion, J., & Todnem, G. (1991). A process for personal theory building. *Educational Leadership, 48*(7), 14-16.

Kitchener, K., & King, P. (1981). Reflective judgment concepts of justification and their relationship to age and education. *Journal of Applied Developmental Psychology, 2*(2), 89-116.

Krest, M. (1990, February). Adapting the portfolio to meet students' needs. *The English Journal,* pp. 29-34.

Lasley, T. (1992, March). *Teacher reflection: Perspectives on the literature.* Paper presented at the 1992 AACTE National Conference, Chicago.

Mills, R. P. (1989). Portfolios capture rich array of student performance. *The School Administrator, 46*(11), 8-11.

Min, H. (1994, May/June). Professional portfolio: Why you should start one now. *Instructor,* p. 50.

Murphy, S., & Smith, M. A. (1990). Talking about portfolios. *The Quarterly, 12*(2).

Pascal, C. E., & Wilburn, M. T. (1978). *A mini-guide to preparing a teaching dossier* (Ontario Universities newsletter). Ontario, Canada: Ontario Universities Program for Instructional Development.

Posner, C. (1985). *Field experience: A guide to reflecive teaching.* New York: Longman.

Ross, P. D. (1989). First steps in developing a reflective approach. *Journal of Teacher Education, 40*(2), 20-30.

Seldin, P. (1991). *The teaching portfolio.* Bolton, MA: Anker.

Shepard, L. A. (1989). Why we need better assessment. *Reading Teacher, 42,* 4-9.

Tyler, R. W. (1942). General statement on evaluation. *Journal of Educational Research, 35,* 492-501.

Valencia, S. (1990). A portfolio approach to classroom reading assessment: The why's, what's, and how's. *Reading Teacher, 43,* 338-340.

Valencia, S. W., Pearson, P. D., Peters, C. W., & Wixson, K. K. (1989). Theory and practice in statewide reading assessment: Closing the gap. *Educational Leadership, 46*(7), 57-63.

Van Manen, M. (1977). Linking ways of knowing with ways of being practical. *Curriculum Inquiry, 12*(6), 1-12.

Vavrus, L. (1990). Putting portfolios to the test. *Instructor, 100*(1), 48-63.

Wiggins, G. (1989). A true test: Toward more authentic and equitable assessment. *Phi Delta Kappan, 7,* 703-713.

Wellington, B. (1991). The promise of reflective practice. *Educational Leadership, 48,* 4-5.

Wolf, D. P. (1989a). Opening up assessment. *Educational Leadership, 46,* 24-39.

Wolf, D. P. (1989b). Portfolio assessment: Sampling student work. *Educational Leadership, 46*(7), 35-39.

CORWIN
PRESS

**The Corwin Press logo**—a raven striding across an open book—represents the happy union of courage and learning. We are a professional-level publisher of books and journals for K–12 educators, and we are committed to creating and providing resources that embody these qualities. Corwin's motto is "Success for All Learners."